# THE EVERYTHING KIDS'® BOOK OF OUTRAGEOUS FACTS

Explore the most fantastic, extraordinary,
and unbelievable truths about your world!

**Beth L. Blair and Jennifer A. Ericsson**

Adamsmedia
Avon, Massachusetts

PUBLISHER  Karen Cooper

DIRECTOR OF ACQUISITIONS AND INNOVATION  Paula Munier

MANAGING EDITOR, EVERYTHING SERIES  Lisa Laing

COPY CHIEF  Casey Ebert

ACQUISITIONS EDITOR  Kate Powers

SENIOR DEVELOPMENT EDITOR  Brett Palana-Shanahan

EDITORIAL ASSISTANT  Ross Weisman

An Everything® Series Book.
Everything® and everything.com® are registered trademarks of F+W Media, Inc.

Published by Adams Media, a division of F+W Media, Inc.
57 Littlefield Street, Avon, MA 02322. U.S.A.
www.adamsmedia.com

ISBN 10: 1-4405-2849-7
ISBN 13: 978-1-4405-2849-1
eISBN 10: 1-4405-2992-2
eISBN 13: 978-1-4405-2992-4

Printed by RR Donnelley, Owensville, MO, USA.
September 2011

10  9  8  7  6  5  4  3  2  1

This publication is designed to provide accurate and authoritative information with regard to the
subject matter covered. It is sold with the understanding that the publisher is not engaged in ren-
dering legal, accounting, or other professional advice. If legal advice or other expert assistance is
required, the services of a competent professional person should be sought.
—From a Declaration of Principles jointly adopted by a Committee of the
American Bar Association and a Committee of Publishers and Associations

Many of the designations used by manufacturers and sellers to distinguish their products are
claimed as trademarks. When those designations appear in this book and Adams Media was
aware of a trademark claim, the designations have been printed with initial capital letters.

Interior illustrations by Kurt Dolber.
Puzzles by Beth L. Blair.

This book is available at quantity discounts for bulk purchases.
For information, please call 1-800-289-0963.

Visit the entire Everything® series at www.everything.com

# contents

Our universe contains stars, galaxies, planets, space, and us! Although the universe has been around for a long time, scientists think it probably formed very quickly. Because it keeps growing and growing, even the best experts can only guess how big the universe is or what shape it may be. Some people believe there are many different universes. Our universe is a big, big place in outer space!

## Countless Galaxies

Have you ever seen the Milky Way? This collection of stars can be seen all over the world. The Milky Way looks like a ring of milk spilled across the sky. It is a small part of Earth's own Milky Way Galaxy, which contains billions of stars. If you could see the Milky Way from another galaxy, it would look like a pinwheel that spins around every couple of hundred million years. Other galaxies may look like a racetrack or a splatter of paint. Did you know that if someone gave you a penny and then doubled that amount each day, so that you had 1 penny the first day, 2 the next day, 4 the next day, and so on and so on, you would soon have more money than you could ever spend? The same is true for our galaxies! There are just too many to be counted.

## Round and Round They Go

Do you ever say the sun is "coming up"? It really does seem like the sun is traveling around our earth. The Egyptian astronomer, Ptolemy, thought the same thing almost 2,000 years ago. But the truth was discovered many centuries later, when a stargazer named Copernicus suggested that our planet really circles around the sun! A famous astronomer called Galileo proved it about 400 years ago.

## FUN FACT

### A REALLY LONG NIGHT

One night on Venus lasts almost as long as a year here on Earth. And because it turns so slowly and it is closer to the sun, Venus's temperature can reach almost 900 degrees on the Fahrenheit scale! Not a good place for a Popsicle.

Did you know that while the earth is busy circling around our sun, the sun circles around the center of our galaxy? Yikes! With so many stars and moons and planets moving around in the universe, it is amazing so few things collide.

## You'll Get a "Bang" out of This

Some scientists spend a lot of time trying to figure out how the universe was formed. Have you ever played with a magic grow sponge? You add a drop of water to a little capsule and quick as a wink, quite a large foam animal appears. Well, some scientists believe the creation of the universe grew quickly and quietly like that, except the capsule was a particle

**FUN FACT**

**STEADY STAR**

The North Star is the only star in the Northern Hemisphere that does not move. On a clear, dark night see if you can find it!

E ✪  H ✰  K ★  N ☆

S ★  T ✪  U ✯  Y ✳

# Picture in the Sky

Use a white gel pen or white crayon to connect the numbers in order. The decoder will help you to spell out the name a Native American tribe used for this group of stars, long before it became known as the Big Dipper.

of matter smaller than a grain of sand and the foam was really a type of super-hot material that grew thousands—maybe millions or billions—of times larger within seconds.

Other scientists believe that there was a big bang like fireworks—only louder—when it happened. That's why the creation of the universe is often called the "Big Bang." Some scientists even believe that they know *when* the Big Bang happened because they have learned how to measure the age of the galaxies. Just imagine! If we were having a birthday party for the universe, we would need around 15 billion candles for the cake!

## The Sun: Too Hot to Handle

Have grown-ups ever told you never to look directly at the bright sun? They're right; it can hurt your eyes. But maybe you have watched the sun as it was setting in the sky. Sometimes it looks as though it is on fire, especially when it is shining through the clouds. The reason it looks that way is because the sun is on fire. Can you guess how hot the fire at the center of the sun is? It is more than 25 million degrees on the Fahrenheit scale! That's 250,000 times hotter than the hottest summer day at your favorite amusement park. More bad news for Popsicles! But what may surprise you even more is there are many stars in the universe that are thousands of times hotter than the sun.

Have you ever wished things were a little hotter or cooler here on Earth? Well, scientists believe that our sun's temperature is just right for us. And they think that the sun will keep burning for many billions of years.

# The Big Bucket

Saturn is huge but weighs so little that it could float in a bucket of water. Complete the equations to learn how big this bucket would need to be!

| 5 | 12 | 1 | 7 | 15 |
|---|----|---|---|----|
| +3 | -7 | +3 | -4 | +1 |
| -4 | +2 | +6 | -2 | -12 |
| +3 | -3 | -2 | +8 | +4 |

*The bucket would have to be more than this many miles wide!*

## AMAZING ASTRONOMY

*The main rings of Saturn stretch more than a hundred thousand miles across space, but guess what? They are only 500 feet thick! That's like covering a soccer field with a single thickness of newspaper!*

5

## Sun-sational Things

Have you ever seen a rainbow in the sky? Sometimes you can spot one if it rains right after a sunrise, or just before a sunset, and then the sun comes back out. Do you know what causes the brilliant colors? It's the sun shining through the moisture in the air after the rain has stopped.

Another fun thing to watch for is sundogs. Sundogs look like colored lines that curve around the sun. The best time to spot them is when the sun is not too far above the horizon. Sundogs get their color from ice particles that are floating in the air.

What other sun-sational things might you see? What if you stood on top of a mountain? Well, if the sun shined from behind you, and the clouds filled with rain below you, you might see a silhouette of your head on those clouds! Your head's shadow might even have a halo surrounding it, just like the moon does at times.

Of course, these strange sightings, which are called "the glory," are very rare. But maybe you could try it on a plane! If you sit in a window seat away from the sun and then watch closely, you may see the silhouette of your plane on the clouds below, with colored rings around it!

## Earth Is Juuuuust Right!

Do you remember the story about the three bears? Goldilocks kept looking until she found a place that was just right for her. Well, you don't have to search very far to find the perfect place for you, because you and all your friends live on it. From space, our planet looks like a big blue-and-white marble. Astronauts are always dazzled to see just how lucky we are to have all those white, fluffy clouds and all that water!

People use water every day for all kinds of things, like taking a bath or watering their lawn. Water can also be used for fun. You can take a trip to the beach, canoe down a river, or ski down a mountain. And of course we need it to grow the fruits and veggies we eat!

Astronomers have discovered there are other planets orbiting stars in distant galaxies, but they don't think we could live on any of them. Although many of the other planets in our solar system have mountains, sunrises, and sunsets, they don't have air or water. Do you think they ever did?

One of the biggest mysteries in space is why Earth is the only planet in our solar system—and maybe even the whole universe—that can support life. What makes a planet "just right"? How many answers can you think of? Here are just a few.

- Our sun creates enough gravity to hold all the planets in orbit. That means the earth travels around the sun in the same path all the time so we don't dash off into space or crash into another planet. The other planets stay on their paths, too!
- The earth is just the right distance from our sun to warm us up without burning us up. The other planets are more Papa and Mama Bear's bowls of porridge: Too hot! Too cold!
- The earth turns every day, so everyone gets a turn to warm up and enjoy some sunshine (well, when it isn't pouring or snowing outside!).
- The earth is tipped a little, so it has seasons. No freezing or roasting!

## FUN FACT

### MONKEY BUSINESS

Although there were no people on the first missions into space, Russian satellites called Sputniks carried dogs, rodents, and even plants. Later, the United States and other countries sent monkeys and other small animals into space. And before all this happened, fruit flies were placed on board rockets, along with rye and cotton seeds! You can think about that amazing flight whenever an insect's bugging you!

## Our Neighbor the Moon

What do you see when you look at the moon? Is it a man's face or does it look more like some type of animal? Many people think they see the man in the moon. Others say they see something else, like a cow, which may have started the whole cow jumping over the moon story.

Okay, so you certainly couldn't jump over the moon like the cow in the nursery rhyme. But did you know that you could jump six times higher off the ground if you lived on the moon? With one small jump, you could probably touch the roof of your house!

# Crazy Moon

A long time ago, people used the Latin word for moon (luna) to create a new word to describe someone they believed had been made crazy by the rays of the full moon. The crazy thing is that we still use this word today! The decoder will help you figure out this common word.

A N
C O
I T
L U

So, just how is that possible? Well, the moon is not only smaller than the earth, but it is made of much lighter materials. That means its gravity is a lot weaker!

Before astronauts landed on the moon, many people thought the moon was made of green cheese. Imagine their surprise when they discovered that what they thought was cheese was really a layer of powdery soil with scattered rocks (which scientists call *regolith*).

**DID YOU KNOW?**

The tire tracks and footprints that astronauts left on the moon will be visible forever? There's no wind on the moon to blow them away!

## Rings and Craters

If you like to look at the moon, you may have noticed from time to time something that looks like a halo or ring around the moon. Sometimes the ring is white, while other times it looks like a faint rainbow. A ring around the moon is caused by light shining through the moisture in the atmosphere, just like the rainbows you see here on Earth. Some people believe that this means that rain or snow is on the way.

Some scientists think that some of the rings on the moon are actually circles of ice in some of the craters. They believe the ice never melts there, because the sun's rays never reach that part of the moon. Your Popsicle wouldn't melt there!

The dark places on the moon are called *mares* or *seas*. Would you believe that at first, astronomers thought the moon's craters were filled with water like the earth's oceans? For years people have been trying to solve the mystery of what caused these craters and why there are so many of them. They may have been caused by meteors that crashed into the surface of the moon.

There are thousands of craters on the side of the moon that we can see. Over time astronomers have given names to most of them. Some actually have common names like Mary

**DID YOU KNOW?**

Golf is the only sport that has been played on the moon. In 1971, astronaut Alan Shepard, commander of the Apollo 14 mission, used a Wilson six-iron head attached to a lunar sample scoop handle to hit golf balls.

## FUN FACT

### HOT AND COLD

One day on the moon is equal to about two weeks here on Earth. The same is true for its night. Such long days and nights cause the moon to get very hot and then very cold. During the day, it can reach 253 degrees on a Fahrenheit scale, while at night it can drop to -387°. Brrrrrrrrrrrrrrrrrrrrrrrrrr!

## FUN FACT

### ROCKETS AWAY!

Hundreds of years ago, men developed rockets that work a lot like the fireworks that are used every Fourth of July. Extremely large versions of these rockets are used to lift modern spaceships into orbit.

or Melissa, while others use the last name of famous astronomers, like Miller or Minkowski.

The moon's craters are so large they would make the craters here on Earth look very tiny. Some of the craters on the moon are hundreds of miles across, while the ones here on Earth, like the one in Arizona, are less than a mile wide.

## Making Waves

When people go to the ocean, they almost always look for shells on the beach. Did you ever wonder how the shells got there? Well, about every twelve hours the tides rise and fall, sweeping the bottom of the ocean as they go along. The exact times of the tides change every day, depending on the movement of the earth and the moon.

The moon affects many things here on Earth. Scientists like to keep an eye on the patterns and changes so they can predict what they call high tides. Why, you ask? In some places, like the Bay of Fundy off the eastern coast of Canada, the tides can change the level of the water around 50 feet. You wouldn't want to get stranded on the beach with all that water rushing in! Also, high tides during violent storms can wash away sea walls and even homes that were built too close to the shore. Scientists use predictions of tides to make sure everyone stays safe.

You may be wondering this: What has the strength to raise all that water onto the beaches on one side of the earth at high tide, and then pull it back toward the beaches on the other side of the earth at low tide? Although the sun's gravity has some effect, it is the gravity of the moon that has so much pull on the earth's surface—even though the moon is hundreds of thousands of miles away!

## It's a Planetary Race!

Let's talk about Venus for a moment. Some people think of Venus as a type of twin to Earth. Here are some ways they're alike:

- Venus has a similar shape and size to Earth.
- Venus is also the closest planet to Earth.
- Even though Venus spins backward, it still orbits the sun in the same direction as the rest of the planets, including Earth.

Did you also know that planets act a little bit like racecars? In fact, the planets in our solar system orbit the sun like racecars going around a track. Like racecars, planets don't orbit in a perfect circle, either. In fact, as the planets near the sun they slow down. Then they speed up as they move away. A planet that is close to the sun takes much less time to complete an orbit than one that is far away. How long does it take for each planet to orbit the sun?

- Mercury is the fastest: almost 88 days, which is just less than 3 months.
- Venus takes almost 3 times as long as Mercury: 224 days, which is about 3 seasons here on Earth.
- Earth's orbit takes 365 days. One whole year!

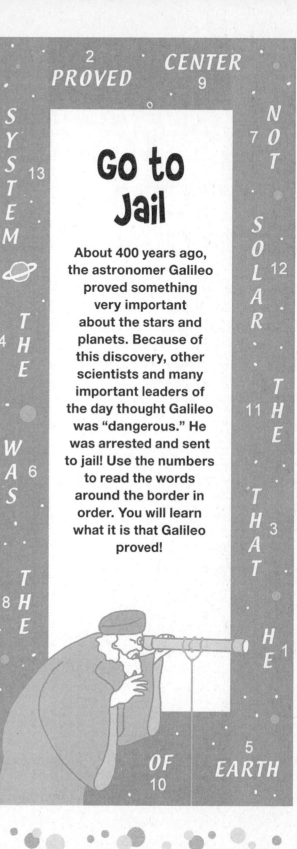

## Go to Jail

About 400 years ago, the astronomer Galileo proved something very important about the stars and planets. Because of this discovery, other scientists and many important leaders of the day thought Galileo was "dangerous." He was arrested and sent to jail! Use the numbers to read the words around the border in order. You will learn what it is that Galileo proved!

Border words with numbers: 2 PROVED, CENTER 9, SYSTEM 13, NOT 7, SOLAR 12, THE 4, THE 11, WAS 6, THAT 3, THE 8, HE 1, OF 10, EARTH 5

## FUN FACT

### LIGHT AS A FEATHER

Saturn has been losing helium from its atmosphere and gaining it in the center of the planet. Astronomers have decided it is raining helium inside the planet, making it sort of like a large helium balloon.

## FUN FACT

### TIME WARP!

Some scientists believe there are places in space where time is distorted or warped. One place they believe a time warp may exist is around a black hole. Because no one has ever been there they can only guess what might happen!

◆ Mars needs about twice as long as Earth to make an orbit: 680 days.

◆ Jupiter takes close to 12 years. That's about the average life span of a dog!

◆ Saturn takes almost 30 years! Wow: long enough for you to grow up and buy your own house!

◆ It takes about 85 years before Uranus returns to its original place in space. Many great-grandparents are 85 years old!

◆ Finally, at the end of its race, Neptune completes its orbit in roughly 165 years. That's twice as long as most people live!

Remember, thanks to the sun's gravity, all of the planets stay in their orbit. And unlike racecars, the planets don't really bunch up as they round the track.

## Mysterious Black Holes

Maybe you've seen a whirlpool in the bathtub before, when the water drains out. Do you know what powers a whirlpool? Gravity does! Well, a black hole is like a whirlpool in space. It's so powerful, it can drag any stars that pass close enough to their destruction. Yikes!

A black hole's gravity is so strong, even light cannot escape from it. This means it's not possible to see a black hole from Earth. In fact, to be able to find a black hole, astronomers must look for its effect on other objects in the sky.

Where would you look for the nearest black hole? Many of the stars in other galaxies appear to be orbiting around a huge, empty space. Maybe this is also what keeps Earth's Milky Way Galaxy spinning around.

# CHAPTER 2

# Amazing Animals

The world is full of wild and wonderful creatures. Some live on land, some live in the ocean, and some may even live in your house. Some animals fly, some slither, and some swim, and some can run as fast as your mom or dad can drive a car! Each animal is fascinating and unique.

## Animals of All Sorts

The animal kingdom is vast. It includes the tiniest beetle and the giant blue whale in the ocean. It includes sponges, worms, insects, fish, lizards, frogs, birds, tigers, and even you!

Backbones make a big difference to biologists who classify life forms. Invertebrates have no backbone. Vertebrates do. Some invertebrates are soft and squishy. Earthworms and jellyfish are two examples. Other invertebrates have an outer covering. Shrimp, snails, and clams have shells, for example. Insects have a hard substance, called *chitin,* covering their bodies. The chitin holds their inner organs together and protects them.

Fish are animals with backbones. Some, like sharks, live in seawater. Others, like trout, have freshwater homes. Fish absorb oxygen from the water through their gills. They reproduce by laying eggs.

Amphibians are also vertebrates. They change form as they mature. A frog, for example, begins its life by swimming around as a tadpole. As it matures, it begins to grow legs. When it's ready, the adult frog hops out of the pond to live on land. When it's time to reproduce, frogs lay eggs in water. The eggs will hatch into new tadpoles.

Reptiles are vertebrates too. They hatch from eggs and breathe air into their lungs. Scales cover their bodies. Snakes, alligators, and lizards are examples of reptiles.

Birds are animals of a different feather altogether. Most birds fly by flapping their wings, although some, like penguins

**FUN FACT**

### IT'S AN ANIMAL PLANET!

Scientists have discovered over 9,000 species of birds, 4,000 species of mammals, 6,000 reptiles, 4,000 amphibians, and 4,500 fish. And those are just the animals with backbones! Nature's diversity is truly amazing!

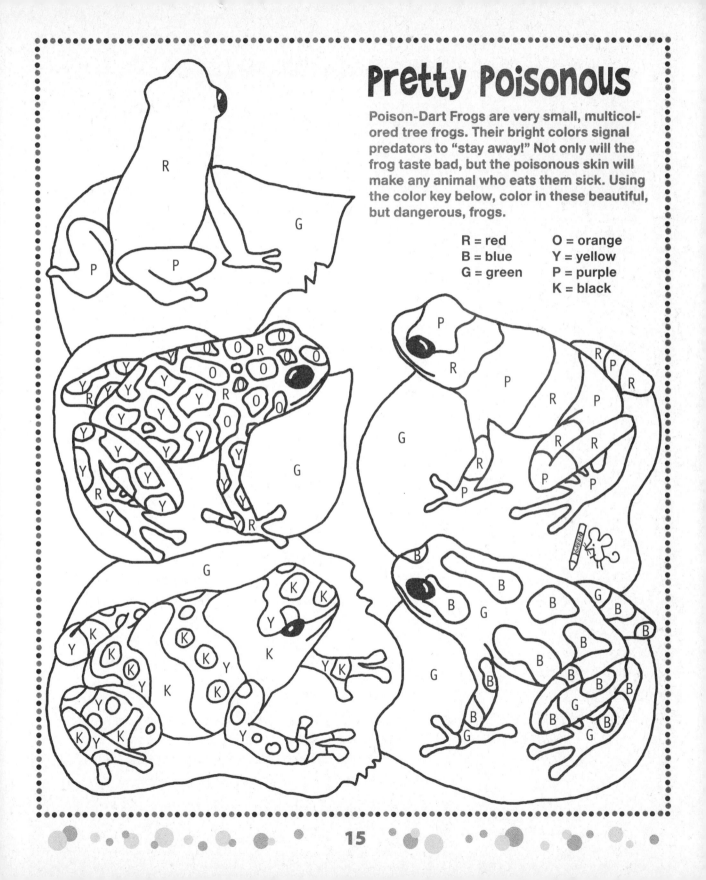

# Pretty Poisonous

Poison-Dart Frogs are very small, multicolored tree frogs. Their bright colors signal predators to "stay away!" Not only will the frog taste bad, but the poisonous skin will make any animal who eats them sick. Using the color key below, color in these beautiful, but dangerous, frogs.

R = red      O = orange
B = blue     Y = yellow
G = green    P = purple
K = black

## DID YOU KNOW? · · · · · · · ·

The chameleon is an odd creature. Its tongue is as long as its body. And its eyes can focus separately to watch two objects at once. Talk about multitasking!

and ostriches, do not fly. Birds' beaks, feet, and bodies seem to come in all shapes and sizes. Young birds hatch from eggs.

Mammals are another class of vertebrates. Mammals have hair on their bodies instead of scales or feathers. Also, unlike other animals, almost all mammals are born alive, not hatched from eggs. Animal mothers nurse their babies with milk from their mammary glands. Dogs, tigers, chimps, horses, and rabbits are examples of mammals. You are a mammal too!

Fish, amphibians, and reptiles are all cold-blooded. This means that their bodies are the same temperature as the area around them. Birds and mammals, on the other hand, are warm-blooded. Their bodies control their own temperature. Your normal temperature is 98.6°F.

## FUN FACT

### SEEING SPOTS

Giraffes are the tallest living animals, standing as high as 20 feet! You wouldn't think a creature this tall could easily disappear, but giraffes can! Their spots are the secret. These brown blotches blend in with the moving shadows from the tall, thin trees found where the giraffes live.

## Chains, Webs, and Pyramids

Only certain single-celled organisms and green plants make their own food. Living things that make their own food are called *primary producers*. Any living thing that can't make its own food must get it from elsewhere.

If an organism feeds on something that made its own food, it is called a *primary consumer*. Many primary consumers are, in turn, eaten by other organisms, which are called *secondary* or *tertiary* (third-level) *consumers*.

Here's an example of a simple *food chain:* Grass makes its own food through photosynthesis, which is eaten by a zebra, which is killed and eaten by a lion. Another example is grass, which is eaten by a field mouse, which is eaten by an owl. Still another example is plankton in the ocean, which is eaten by krill (a shrimp-like animal), which is in turn eaten by a whale.

Not all relationships in nature are so simple. Instead of a food chain, a *food web* may exist in which species are sometimes predators and sometimes prey. On the Arctic tundra, for example, caribou graze on lichens and plants. Summer mosquitoes feed by biting the caribou and other animals. Birds, in turn, eat the mosquitoes and other bugs. But birds may also become food for Arctic wolves. The wolves, in turn, might get bitten by mosquitoes or attacked by a polar bear.

How many of each type of organism is needed to maintain balance in nature? Generally, most areas support far fewer meat-eating animals (carnivores) than plant-eating animals (herbivores). In turn, each plant-eating animal needs many plants to support itself. As a result, scientists sometimes talk about a *food pyramid*. Organisms at the base of the pyramid support all the life forms above them.

## FUN FACT

### VEGGIE LOVERS

There are only two marine animals that feed exclusively on vegetation: the manatee and the dugong. These veggie lovers eat more than 30 pounds of plants in one day!

## Animal Communication

We can't talk to animals like Hugh Lofting's hero in *The Story of Dr. Doolittle*, but animals communicate with each other well enough. Some animals communicate with sound. Others use visual displays. Still others rely on smell or touch.

Just what are the animals "saying"? Animal messages fall into broad categories that get important information across about mating and survival.

### DID YOU KNOW?

Leopards protect their food from other animals by dragging it high up into the trees. A leopard will often leave its prey up in the tree for days and return only when it's hungry!

### "Won't You Be Mine?"

Animals don't send valentines, but they do want to attract mates. So, they draw attention to themselves.

For example, male grasshoppers chirp by stroking their hind legs over their wings. Male fiddler crabs wave their huge claws. Fireflies light up parts of their abdomens on summer nights to form code-like patterns.

Male ruffs and other birds strut back and forth to show off their brightly colored feathers. Some birds, like white gannets,

# many meerkats

Meerkats are tough little animals that live in the Kalahari Desert of southern Africa. Desert life isn't easy, but meerkats have found a good safety system. They live in groups and work together as a team to protect each other, find food, and raise the babies. They all share the work, and they all share the benefits!

If the meerkats here gathered all the numbers hidden in this picture, then divided them equally, what number would each of them be left with?

preen each other. That means they help clean bugs and dirt out of their feathers. Still other birds, like grebes, seem to have mating dances. In a display called *rushing,* grebes look like they're running across the water's surface.

### "I'm Tough"

A male gorilla says "I'm tough!" by using a threat display. The gorilla stands on his hind legs, beats his chest, and yanks at nearby branches. This behavior shows that he is the boss. It can also frighten others so they won't challenge him to a fight. Male baboons show they're in charge by baring their teeth.

A ring-tailed lemur may walk with her long tail held high in the air. The signal shows that she's a leader in the group.

### "Don't Mess with Me"

If a tiger bares its teeth, wrinkles its nose, and sets its ears back, watch out. The tiger is ready to attack if necessary. An aggressive look on a wolf's face can warn other wolves to leave it alone. On the other hand, a wolf with its tail between its legs is saying it doesn't want to challenge another wolf.

Rattlesnakes can bite attackers with their fangs, but then they've used up all their venom, so they can't attack prey to eat right away. So sometimes when they're threatened, rattle-snakes just shake their rattles—a group of bony pieces at the end of their tails. The rattle noise warns off their enemies.

### "Watch Out!"

While meerkats hunt and dig in southern Africa's deserts, at least one member of the group keeps lookout. If danger comes near, the meerkat barks loudly. Its barking sends the others rushing to their burrows. Likewise, the Arctic ground squirrel's

**DID YOU KNOW?**

Whales sing as a call to mates, a way to communicate, and also just for fun! After a period of time they get bored of the same whale song and begin to sing a different tune.

loud chirp acts as a warning that an enemy lurks nearby. The sound sends everyone bolting for cover.

### "Keep Out!"

The Klipspringer antelope wipes scent from glands on its face against branches. The scent tells other antelopes to stay away from its territory. Hippos and white rhinos use really smelly scent marking to define their territory. The white rhino sprays urine around. The hippo whirls its tail to fling dung over a wide area. Ewwwww!

## Spotlight on: Sharks

If you decided to hold an Olympic contest tomorrow, the shark family would probably win most of the events. The blue shark is used to swimming very long distances because it travels thousands of miles each year to migrate, and it would probably win the swim marathon. The mako shark could win the medal for the fastest swimmer because it reaches speeds of around fifty miles an hour.

The record for deep-sea diving would have to go to the megamouth shark, because it can swim thousands of feet down below the ocean's surface only to travel all the way back up to the top again each night. The megamouth would probably win the title of strongest fish, too, since it is able to support thousands of pounds of water pressure on every inch of its body.

Then there's the thresher shark, which uses its tail like a hockey stick. Imagine the thresher shark joining the great white shark to make a prize-winning team for penguin volleyball. They could bounce those poor little penguins way up in the air just for fun.

Of course, the high-jumping contest would go to the basking shark. Basking sharks, which are as big as houses, spend

**FUN FACT**

### SHARK EGGS

A shark's eggs can hatch inside or outside of the mother. Once the egg hatches, the baby shark might be on its own, out in the ocean. Some hatchlings stay inside the mother waiting for the right time to be born, which can take anywhere from a few months to two years. The length of time depends on the type of shark.

their time jumping up out of the water to get rid of the parasites or pests that cling to them. Can you imagine being famous for trying to get someone or something to quit bugging you?

## Fear Not

What scares a shark? Well, for starters other sharks do and humans do, too. But sharks can also be scared of dolphins. Would you think those cute little playful dolphins could ever frighten a shark? They not only scare sharks; they can also be deadly. Dolphins have actually been known to keep butting their heads against a shark's side until the shark is dead!

Humans are probably the shark's greatest enemy. When a person enters a shark's neighborhood or area, the shark usually tries to give a warning so that the person will leave. Let's say you saw a mako shark swimming toward you, making a figure eight like an Olympic skater. Well, you might think you had nothing to fear—right until it opened its mouth. Mako sharks have teeth that are as big as a grown man's fingers!

Not all sharks give a warning that looks like an event from the Olympics. To let you know that it means business, the gray reef shark prefers to hunch its back like an angry cat, scrunch up its nose, and push its pectoral fins downward as though it were putting on its brakes.

Most sharks have their own way to threaten you before they attack. If you continue to approach them, they further warn you with their eyes. One way to know when a shark is not in the mood to play is when its eyelid, the nictitating membrane, starts to rise from the bottom of its eye. This is the shark's way of letting you know there may be a fight. The nictitating membrane protects the shark's eyes so its victim can't damage them. These membranes work like the wipers on a car's windshield. They clean the shark's eyes as they pass over them.

## FUN FACT

### NOT A CUTE COOKIE

Why would a creature with a name like the cookie-cutter shark make whales, dolphins, or other sharks worried? Especially since these sharks are less than two feet long? What the other animals don't like is how a cookie-cutter will swim up to their sides, grab on to them, bite down, and then spin themselves around until they leave a small hole in the animal's body. Ouch!

## DID YOU KNOW? ........

A shark always has a row of smaller teeth developing behind its front teeth. Eventually the smaller teeth move forward, like a conveyor belt, and the front teeth fall out.

Some folks say it's important to "Look people right in the eye when you talk to them." With sharks and other animals—and even some humans!—this isn't always such a great idea! In some cases, looking a person or an animal in the eye can also mean you're looking for a fight. Making eye contact with a shark or any other wild animal is never a good plan.

### Was It a Monster?

The size of a fish changes depending on its environment. In other words, if you place a small goldfish in a small bowl, it will stay almost the same size. But if you put the same fish in a large pond, over time, that fish will become enormous! Do you think that living in the ocean, with all that water, has allowed some of the sharks to grow to their gigantic size? If you could put a baby shark in a small container, would it never get any bigger?

Basking sharks, the second-biggest fish in the ocean, are as big as a house, with a caudal fin or tail large enough

to swat a boat. They got their name because they seem to enjoy basking in the sun. And there's also a mystery about them! Basking sharks seem to disappear during the winter. Where do they go? Well, scientists used satellite tags to track the basking sharks. They discovered that during the winter months, basking sharks spend more time in deeper water to feed on communities of deep-water plankton. So for a while, they cannot be found in their usual spots.

Basking sharks are probably also responsible for many stories of sea serpents and other ocean monsters. Let's imagine a day several hundred years ago, when a beachcomber stumbled across the remains of a basking shark. It was so enormous, he thought he had found an actual sea serpent like the ones in fairy tales! He was sure this proved that monsters really did exist, and he went to tell other people what he had found. Can you imagine how the dorsal fins of this mighty shark could look like a sea serpent, especially when people saw groups of them swimming around offshore?

Was this the first fish story? For years, many fishermen have enjoyed telling tall tales about the huge fish that they supposedly caught. Yet in the stories, somehow these huge fish always get away. You and your friends could write your own fish stories or stories of serpents and other sea monsters. Make them as far-fetched as possible, such as "The fish was so long, it could tie itself in knots." If you look on the Internet and search for the names of different sharks, you may get some good ideas for your stories when you see exactly how strange some of the real-life ocean dwellers really are!

## FUN FACT

### NOW THAT'S HEAVY

One whale shark weighs as much as three school buses, about 15 tons. A basking shark can weigh even more: as much as 19 tons. Luckily, both types of sharks are filter feeders, not predators!

## Catching a Shark

Greenland sharks, which are almost as long as a minivan, are known as sleeper sharks because they like to lie around and sleep. In fact, the natives of Canada fear them so little that they catch Greenland sharks with a hook and line. Of course, the line they use isn't lightweight like the fishing line you would use for catching trout. These shark hunters use a rope and a chain to prevent the shark from cutting through the line with its teeth. The only problem with fishing this way is that it could be very hard to cut that chain if the shark turned on you and you wanted to get it off the line.

## How Old Are They?

Do you know which animal is one of the oldest creatures on Earth? If you guessed the shark, you're right! They're even older than the dinosaurs!

Sharks have survived for millions of years by following the same cycle of life, just like humans and other animals. They have their babies. The babies grow up, and then they have more babies.

Although the shark family has been around for millions of years, the average shark doesn't live very long. Scientists believe that most of them live only one-fourth as long as humans, but even they don't know for sure. Most sharks seem to live for only about 25 years.

It's not easy to tell how old an adult shark is because they are continually losing their denticles and their teeth. Guessing a young shark's age is a lot easier—some baby sharks' spots change, as well as the size and shape of their teeth. Unless you had a baby shark for a pet and watched it grow up, how would you ever be able to guess how old a shark was? The only way we can really know is by keeping track of some of the sharks that are raised in captivity. Some of these sharks have lived in aquariums for 20 years or more.

## FUN FACT

### DO SHARKS HAVE EARS?

You can't see a shark's ears because they are located down inside of the shark's head. But even though you can't see these inner ears, the shark has excellent hearing and balance because of them. It's even possible that they can hear prey from several miles away!! Shhhhhhhhh!

# Gentle Giants

There are only two marine mammals that feed exclusively on vegetation, eating more than 30 pounds of plants in one day! Answer the clues on each creature to learn its name.

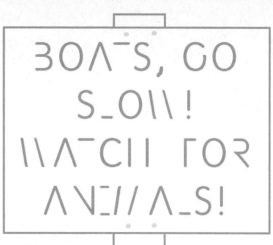

BOATS, GO SLOW! WATCH FOR ANIMALS!

Because they swim slowly and near the surface, these creatures often get hit by boats! Help these two have a safe swim by fixing this sign. Use only straight lines!

grown-up boy | first letter | golf ball stand

past tense of dig | reverse of no | letter before H

## FUN FACT

### NO BONES ABOUT IT

Although there are horses in Australia now, this wasn't always the case. Australia is the only continent on the planet where no horse fossils have ever been found!

## FUN FACT

### FASCINATING FOUL

In 1945 Lloyd Olsen of Colorado cut the head off a chicken. The chicken, named Mike, lived for 18 months without a head. The chicken became a celebrity and even went on tour.

## Spotlight on: Horses

Have your grandparents ever said "Ah, horsefeathers," when they thought you were fibbing to them? Did you know some horses really do have feathers? They're those big tufts of hair that are on the back of the legs of a Clydesdale (and a few other types of horses).

Do you think horses have toes? You probably know that each hoof is like one great big toe, but does a horse have any more toes than this one? If you have access to a horse, and an adult who is able to help you, feel the bump on the back of the horse's front leg where your elbow would be. Then check the bump under the feathers on the backside of the hoof. These bumps are called *chestnuts* and *ergots*. Don't they feel like toes? At one time, millions of years ago, they were!

### Going to the Dentist

Have you ever wondered if horses have teeth like ours that need to be cleaned by a dentist or brushed twice a day? People can tell a horse's age by its teeth, and they can also tell your age by looking at your teeth! Unlike human teeth, horses' teeth develop sharp edges, so they need to be smoothed twice a year by a veterinarian, who is also their dentist. This is called *floating*. "Okay, Mr. Horse, open wide, please!"

A horse's teeth continue to grow throughout the horse's life, which means the oldest section needs to be filed off each year. Because the base of each horse's tooth is always new, the teeth should never rot. No cavities, no dentures!

How does a veterinarian file a horse's teeth? Vets use a really large file, sometimes an electric one. And instead of setting up a dental office for horses, the vet either comes out to the stable or the owners bring the horse to the vet. Of course, like humans, horses can feel a bit nervous about all this. Many

## FUN FACT

### HEAVY HORSES

Did you know there are horses that weigh over one and a half tons? That is close to a compact car. Horses weren't always this size, but over time, several breeds have grown larger.

wild horses need to have a shot to calm them down before the vet can get to work. But if a horse is tame or trained, it is much easier to get it to do what you want and to give it the care it needs—hopefully without a shot!

## Do Horses Have Tusks?

Most horses do have tusks! Some horses' tusks just don't come through their gums. Horses' gums are never completely filled with teeth. They have empty spots between their front and back teeth that are called *bars*. You can reach through these openings to rub their tongues or you can place the bit of their bridle in this space. Some horses also have teeth called *wolf teeth*, which are like small pegs, but they don't usually get to keep them. The veterinarian usually takes out the horse's wolf teeth because they get in the way! When you try to put the bit into the horse's mouth, the wolf teeth are right in front of the first molars in the horse's jaw.

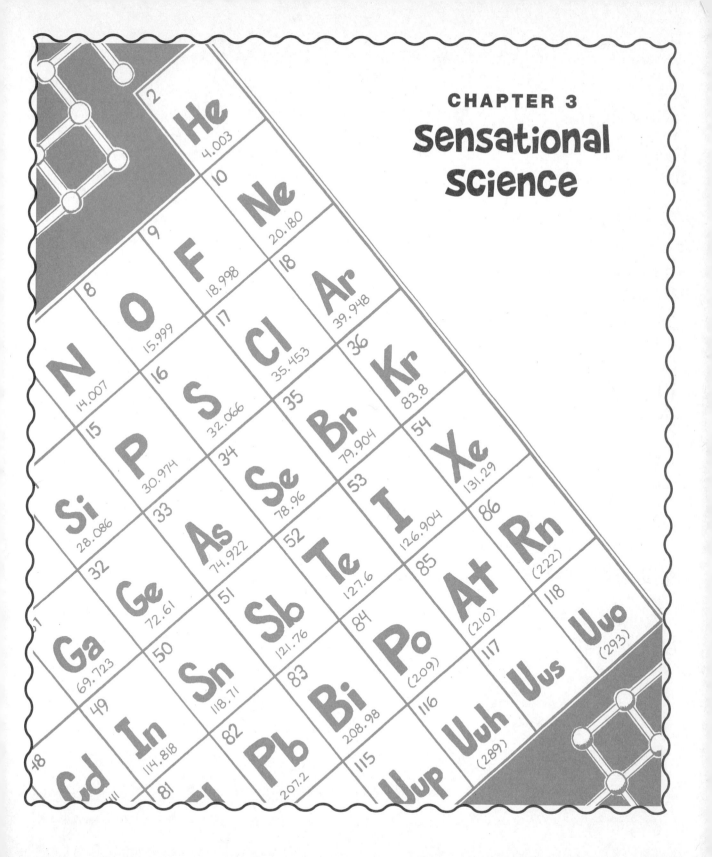

What does it take to be a great scientist? Think of the most famous scientists you know—Isaac Newton, Benjamin Franklin, Louis Pasteur, Albert Einstein, Thomas Edison, Marie Curie, Stephen Hawking, and so on. What do all these people have in common? Well, for one thing, they were all very smart. But there is something else they all had in common that set them apart from the others of their time—their ability to ask questions.

To be a great scientist, you need to be able to look at a problem that hundreds, maybe even thousands, of people have already looked at and could not solve, and ask the question in a new way. Then you take that question and come up with a new way to answer it. That is what made Newton and the others so famous. They were smart *and* curious. They said, "I want to know the answer to this." Could you be the next great scientist? Could you answer a question no one has been able to answer? Absolutely! All you need is something that kids naturally have—curiosity.

## DID YOU KNOW? ⋯⋯⋯

All the matter that makes up the human race could fit in a sugar cube! Atoms are 99.99 percent empty space. If you forced your the atoms together, removing the space between them, a single teaspoon would weigh 5 billion tons; about 10 times the weight of all the humans who are currently alive!

## Biology Experiment: Can You Blow Up a Balloon with a Banana?

Have you ever seen a yucky brown banana? Maybe you forgot to eat it, or it sat on the counter too long. As the fruit ripens, strange and mysterious things seem to happen. In fact, when a banana decomposes—which is a fancy way to say "starts to rot"—bacteria flock to hop on board. Of course, bacteria are so small you can't see them. But not only are they there, they multiply and multiply by eating what's left of the banana.

And then guess what happens? All those little bacteria start to give off gas! Well, it's not a lot of gas, but with enough bacteria present, the gas will inflate a balloon. Your challenge, once you complete this experiment, is to try other overripe fruits to see if they produce the same results.

## FUN FACT

### WHAT KIND OF TREE?

Latex balloons come from the rubber tree, which produces enough sap to make three 10-inch balloons each day.

## Experiment Overview

In this experiment, you will watch as a banana decomposes over time and inflates a balloon. The process is not something you can see, but the effects are unmistakable.

## Materials

- A very ripe banana
- A bowl
- A small-mouth plastic or glass bottle
- An uninflated balloon

## Procedure

1. Peel the banana and mash in it the bowl with a fork until the lumps are gone.
2. Carefully scoop the banana mush into the bottle. This might be a little tricky (and messy!), but with patience, it can be done. (You may also want to try using a plastic knife to scoop the banana mush into the bottle. This may be easier.)
3. Place the balloon over the mouth of the bottle.
4. Place the bottle in a warm, sunny spot and watch the bottle over the course of a few days.
5. Measure the distance around the balloon each day to track the progress of the banana's decay.

## Questions for the Scientist

- What is causing the balloon to inflate?

  _____

- What is happening to the banana?

  _____

- How long did it take for the balloon to begin inflating?

  _____

## Follow-up

Now that you have the procedure down, try mashing other ripe fruit (like apples, oranges, grapes, melons) and repeating the experiment. By comparing the growth rate of each fruit's balloon, you will be able to determine which fruit decays the fastest.

## Clean-up

Be sure to clean up this experiment near a sink or somewhere outside. It's going to be pretty stinky! Carefully throw away all your materials before starting over.

## Chemistry Experiment: Can You Push an Egg into a Bottle Without Touching It?

Do you know what happens when you get a hole in a tire in your bicycle? The air starts to leak out. Time to find a repair kit and a tire pump or call for a ride home!

But have you ever wondered *why* the air leaks out? Well, air has a very interesting behavior. It always flows from high pressure to low pressure. In this experiment, you'll be placing a hard-boiled egg between high pressure (the outside air) and low pressure (the air inside a bottle). You will discover that air wants so badly to get inside the bottle, it will push away anything in its way—even a hard-boiled egg! This is how you'll get the egg in.

But remember, for this to work, the pressure outside the bottle has to be more than the pressure inside the bottle. How can you lower the pressure inside the bottle? By placing lit matches inside the bottle. The matches will burn until the oxygen inside the bottle has been used up. This will lower the air pressure. Then, as the outer air pushes into the bottle, the egg will slide in.

### Experiment Overview

Air has the ability to make objects move into and out of places that they otherwise would not fit. In this experiment, you will force a hard-boiled egg into a bottle without touching the egg.

**DID YOU KNOW?** ·······

Animal explosions are real, and can happen for some strange reasons. On 2004, a buildup of gas inside a decomposing sperm whale caused it to burst in Taiwan. Several toads in Europe exploded in 2005 as they puffed themselves up to look bigger. Looks like they went too far!

## Materials

◆ An adult (to handle the matches!)
◆ Wide-mouth glass bottle (20–32-ounce glass juice bottles will work but make sure that the egg is just barely too big. If the opening is too small, the egg will probably get stuck.)
◆ 1 hard-boiled egg with the shell removed
◆ 3 matches

## Procedure

### Insertion

**1.** Place the hard-boiled egg on the mouth of the bottle. It should sit comfortably without falling off. You may try to push the egg into the bottle to verify that it does not easily fit.

**2.** Remove the egg and place three lit matches into the bottle. Use matches only with adult supervision!

**3.** Quickly replace the egg on the mouth of the bottle, effectively sealing the top of the bottle.

**4.** Watch as the matches go out and the egg is pulled down into the bottle.

### Removal

**1.** Turn the bottle upside down so the egg falls into the opening without coming out. Blow into the opening. (It is recommended to have an adult do this part.)

**2.** As the pressure inside the bottle increases, the egg should be pushed out of the bottle into the adult's mouth.

## Questions for the Scientist

◆ Why did the egg get pushed into the bottle?

_____

◆ What did the burning matches have to do with this experiment?

_____

◆ What are some other examples of air flowing from high pressure to low pressure?

_____

## EUREKA!

Archimedes is famous for shouting "Eureka—I've found it!" before jumping up from his bath and running through town when he discovered his principle of buoyancy.

## Physics Experiment: Why Do Boats Float?

According to the Archimedes Principle, boats float because water pushes up on them with a force equal to their weight. This is called *buoyancy*. You can take a material (such as clay), and form it into a shape that will sink. Or you can take that same amount of clay and form it into a boat that will float. You, and boat designers around the world, have to determine what shape produces the most buoyancy. Once you do that, you're ready to float your boat and even take some cargo on board!

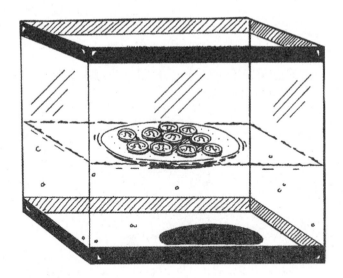

## Experiment Overview

Using pieces of modeling clay, pennies, and paper clips, you can explore how size and shape affect a boat's ability to float. How much weight can your boat hold? Which design works best? Let's grab some materials and see!

## Materials

- Tank of water (aquarium) or large mixing bowl filled with water
- Modeling clay
- Pennies

## Procedure

1. Roll a lump of clay about the size of your palm into a ball and drop it into the water. Observe what happens to the clay.
2. Remove the clay and mold it into several different shapes until it floats. Then place pennies in your boat until it finally sinks. Keep track of how many pennies it held.
3. Test several successful shapes to see which holds the most pennies before sinking.

## Questions for the Scientist

- Which clay boat held more weight?

_____

- Why did some boats hold more weight than others?

_____

- Does this idea apply to large ships that cross oceans and carry thousands of tons of cargo? How do they stay afloat if they are made of metal?

_____

- Why don't people float like your boats did?

_____

## Earth Science Experiment: How Do Icicles Grow?

Icicles can form only under special conditions. It must be cold enough for water to freeze, but there must also be a way for ice to melt so it drips. This is why icicles are commonly found along the edge of the roof of a house. The warmth of the house can cause snow on the roof to melt and drip to the edge of the house. As the water drips off the side, some of it freezes. Later, even more drops run down the frozen droplets and freeze when they reach the end. In this fashion, the icicle grows drop by drop.

In caves, stalactites and stalagmites grow in the same way. A *stalactite* is a solid formation of minerals that hangs from the ceiling of a cave. A *stalagmite* is a similar object the forms on the bottom of a cave.

The only difference between icicles and these amazing cave formations is that the water that drips in the cave doesn't freeze. Instead, each drop of water leaves behind a tiny amount of a mineral called *calcite*. Eventually, enough calcite builds up and hardens that a stalactite forms. Stalagmites are formed when some of the calcite falls to the ground and gradually builds up from the floor. After a long time, the stalactites that grow from the ceiling meet up with the stalagmites growing up from the floor and a column is formed.

**DID YOU KNOW?** • • • • • • • •

The world's largest stalactite is 26.9 feet long and can be found in The Jeita Grotto in Lebanon.

### Experiment Overview

In this experiment, you'll explore the formation of icicles by building stalactites—towers of rock-hard minerals usually found in caves deep in the earth. Remember, the process by which they form is very similar to how icicles form. You'll be using a common drugstore product called *Epsom salts,* and you'll get to watch the "icicles" grow right before your very eyes!

## Materials

- Large glass that you can use for mixing
- Water
- Small spoon
- Box of Epsom salts (available at a local drugstore)
- 2 small glasses
- Thick string or a piece of cloth that will absorb water easily

## Procedure

1. Fill the large glass with water and slowly stir in the Epsom salts until you cannot dissolve any more (some of the salt remains and won't dissolve).
2. Fill each small glass with half of the solution you have prepared.
3. Place an end of the string in each glass and let the middle of the string hang between the glasses.
4. Watch your stalactite and stalagmite grow over the next few days. Measure it each day and keep track of its growth.

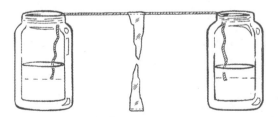

## Questions for the Scientist

- Which of your cones is the stalactite and which is the stalagmite?

_____

- How fast did your stalactite grow (how many inches per day)?

_____

- Did the process go faster at one time than another during your experiment?

_____

- If you live where it's cold enough for icicles, how do you suppose they form?

_____

- How could you prevent icicles from forming on your house?

_____

## Follow-up

Do you think this experiment will work with other substances? Try baking soda, table salt, sugar, and so on.

## Human Body Experiment: How Can You Taste Different Flavors?

Did you know that your tongue has thousands of tiny taste buds on it? Each one reacts to a certain kind of taste. Taste buds that respond to the same taste are grouped together in certain locations on your tongue. So you will always taste salty foods in certain places, sweet foods in other places, and sour and bitter foods in still other places, no matter what food you are eating!

### Experiment Overview

In this experiment you will place different food items on different places of your tongue to determine which taste buds can sense which flavors. You'll test sweet, sour, bitter, and salty. Feeling hungry yet?

### Materials

◆ Cotton swabs
◆ Small bowls containing the following:

  • Lemon juice
  • Water
  • Sugar
  • Table salt
  • Instant coffee

◆ A diagram of the tongue (see next page)
◆ Marking pen

## Procedure

1. Dip a cotton swab in the lemon juice and spread it around your mouth.
2. Mark on the diagram below where on your tongue you sensed this sour taste.
3. Dip a second cotton swab in water and then into the sugar. Spread enough around in your mouth so that you can tell where your tongue senses this sweet taste.
4. Repeat this same procedure with the salt and the instant coffee (a bitter taste).
5. Record on the diagram the places where you sensed each taste.
6. Check your diagram to make sure that you have covered each part of the tongue. If you missed one, repeat the experiment to find the taste sensed by that part of the tongue.

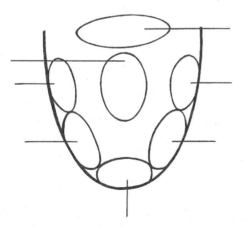

## Questions for the Scientist

◆ Which parts of the tongue responded to sour?

_____

◆ Which parts of the tongue responded to sweet?

_____

◆ Which parts of the tongue responded to salty?

_____

◆ Which parts of the tongue responded to bitter?

_____

◆ Does your diagram of the tongue explain the location of sores after eating too much sugar?

_____

## Follow-up

Try other foods that you know to be in one of these four categories. When you eat them, try to see if you can taste them on the part of your tongue that you marked in this experiment. Try plugging your nose and testing for these four tastes. Does your nose affect your ability to recognize tastes?

Want to watch some sports? Just turn on the television or walk to the park. Chances are, you'll see lots of different games being played. But all of these sports had to start somewhere! Here we'll take a look at some fun facts and the origins of baseball, football, and soccer.

## Baseball

Baseball has been played for more than 150 years! The game became well known around the United States during and after the Civil War, in the 1860s. Back then, pitchers threw underhanded, no one had gloves, and the ball was softer than what we know as a baseball today. Also, the bases were 42 paces (probably about 120 feet) from each other—but it was baseball. The idea was to hit the ball, get from base to base safely, and score runs before getting three outs in your team's turn at bat.

Amateur teams were formed, and they played until the first team scored 21 runs, which at that time only took a few innings. In 1857 someone introduced the idea of playing a game with 9 innings, the bases were placed 90 feet apart, and more rules were changed.

### The First Professional Teams

As far back as the 1860s there were *barnstorming teams*, which were teams that went from city to city playing each other. At first, everyone just played for fun and volunteered their time for free. But eventually, players took the game more seriously and asked to be paid. The first of these teams to be made up entirely of paid players was the Cincinnati Red Stockings of 1869. That first professional team's record was 57–0. No one ever beat them!

In 1871 the National Association of Professional Baseball Players was formed with 9 teams. The Philadelphia Athletics were the first champions, winning 22 and losing only 7. In 1876 the National League was formed. Many players from the original association became part of this new league, including "Cap" Anson, who was considered one of the game's first star players.

Through the 1880s and 1890s, several other leagues, including the American Association, the Players League, and a minor league called the Western League, began. All except the Western League failed.

### Statistics

Math is really important—even in baseball! More than any other sport, statistics are very much a part of this game. Since the beginning of the sport, fans have wanted to know who had the most hits, who made the error, who got the win, and so on. Home run totals, batting averages, wins, strikeouts—they are all a central part of baseball's popularity. Sometimes when a player was on the verge of breaking a record, like when Cal Ripken Jr. played in his 2,131st game, or when Hank Aaron hit home run number 715, the individual achievements of the players got more attention than the ballgame! That's part of what makes baseball so interesting. Your team may not be doing well, like the Giants in 2006, but you might want to watch them anyway, just to see a slugger like Barry Bonds pile up home runs on his way to a record.

# Game Pieces

Baseball is such a familiar game that you might not even need words to describe it! Study the four picture puzzles below and see if you can figure out what baseball play, player, or place they each describe.

**DID YOU KNOW?** ........

Before 1859, umpires sat in a padded rocking chair behind the catcher. Baseball was a much more relaxed game in those days!

There's a stat for everything in baseball. You could probably find the answer to "What pitcher threw the most wild pitches in night games at Wrigley Field in the 1940s?" Okay, so that's a trick question—there were no night games at Wrigley in the 1940s because they had no lights. But the point is that if you love statistics you could probably spend a year looking at baseball statistics and never see the same one twice.

## One-Season Records

*Hitting*

- Most Doubles: Earl Webb 67, Boston Red Sox 1931
- Most Triples: Chief Wilson 36, Pittsburgh Pirates 1912
- Most Home Runs: Barry Bonds 73, San Francisco Giants 2001
- Most Runs Batted In: Hack Wilson 191, Chicago Cubs 1930
- Most Hits: Ichiro Suzuki 262, Seattle Mariners 2004
- Highest Batting Average (500+ Plate Appearances): Hugh Duffy .438, 1894
- Highest Average (500+ Plate Appearances) since 1900: Rogers Hornsby .424, St. Louis Cardinals 1924
- Most Stolen Bases: Rickey Henderson 130, Oakland Athletics 1982

*Pitching*

- Most Wins: Jack Chesbro 41, New York Highlanders 1904
- Most Strikeouts: Nolan Ryan 383, California Angels 1973; Sandy Koufax 382, Los Angeles Dodgers, 1965
- Lowest Earned Run Average: Dutch Leonard 1.01, Boston Red Sox 1914
- Most Shutouts: Grover Alexander 16, Philadelphia Phillies 1916
- Most Saves: Bobby Thigpen 57, Chicago White Sox 1990

**FUN FACT**

**BACK-TO-BACK NO-HITTERS!**

The only pitcher ever to throw no-hitters in 2 starts in a row was Johnny Vander Meer of the Cincinnati Reds in 1938.

## Football

In most countries other than the United States, when people talk about football they mean the game we call soccer. Here in the United States, football actually means football, as in the game you play with a brown, oval-shaped ball.

For most of history, people have played games with balls and goals. At least 500 years ago in England, the game we call soccer developed. In soccer, players try to put a round ball into a goal without using their hands. In the early 1800s, players at the Rugby School in England started cheating. Instead of kicking the ball, they picked it up and ran with it into the goal. Some teams liked to play against the Rugby School—they just tackled whoever picked up the ball! Other teams wanted to play soccer the normal way. Soon two separate forms of the sport were played. In rugby, players were supposed to run with the ball, and defenders were supposed to tackle the ballcarrier to the ground.

### Coming to America

Americans picked up the game of rugby, but every team wanted to play by different rules. In the late 1800s, several colleges and athletic clubs in America played games similar to rugby. East Coast schools such as Princeton, Rutgers, Harvard, and Yale eventually got together to try to make a single set of rules.

By the early 1900s, American rugby had changed enough that you probably could have

# Where's the Player?

Break the Last to First code to read this silly riddle and its silly answer!

hatW si het ifferenced etweenb a ootballf layerp nda a uckd?

. . . . . . . . . . . . . . . . . . .

ou'llY indf neo ni a uddleh, nda het thero ni a uddlep!

## FUN FACT

### EUREKA! IT'S THE 49ERS!

Gold was discovered in California in 1848, and large numbers of gold diggers flocked to the West Coast starting in 1849. The new arrivals were nicknamed 49ers. Nearly 100 years later, the All-America Football League created a franchise in San Francisco, and the team took on the 49ers name. Sourdough Sam, the 49ers mascot, is a cheerful football-loving gold digger.

recognized the game as football. Every play was a running play. Blockers (without much padding) slammed into each other as hard as they could. There were so many injuries, in fact that many people tried to ban the sport. At the personal request of President Teddy Roosevelt, Yale athletic director Walter Camp led a group of people who created a more exciting and less dangerous game than had been played before. It was Camp who insisted that 11 players was the right number for a team. He also invented the idea that the offense had to gain yardage to get a first down. Most important, Camp revolutionized football by inventing the forward pass.

## College Football

College—not pro—football was the popular spectator sport through the first half of the 1900s. Colleges throughout the country formed teams, and more and more people started watching and playing football. The college bowl games on New Year's Day were the highlight of each season. In the 1920s, colleges all over the country played football. At that point, professional teams had started playing in the Midwest. Both the pro and college games were well known and well followed. However, football didn't become the big deal that it is now until after the Great Depression and World War II.

## TV Makes Football Popular

In the 1950s, most people could afford TV sets at home. Television networks figured out that people loved to watch football. Televised football made the game even more popular and provided a good deal of money for team owners. The Super Bowl, first played in 1967, became the most important sporting event in America. Fans enjoyed watching their favorite college players competing for many years as professionals. Nowadays, you'll see both college and pro football on TV—college on Saturday, pro on Sunday. Many college teams and almost all pro teams sell out of tickets to their stadiums every week. High schools and youth leagues stage games each week as well, giving more people a chance to play or watch the game.

**DID YOU KNOW?**

Did you know the first football ever used was round?

### The Biggest Event in America: The Super Bowl

The AFL-NFL championship game was named the "Super Bowl" by Chiefs owner Lamar Hunt. Super indeed. After more than 40 years, Super Bowl Sunday is an unofficial national holiday. The game has become much more than just a league championship. Many Americans—at least one-third of the population—watch the game on television, and many people throw parties and watch with their friends and families.

The NFL uses Roman numerals to number the Super Bowls. You may have learned about these in school. Roman numerals use letters to represent numbers: I means 1, V means 5, X means 10, and L means 50. It gets a bit more complicated—IV means 4, while VI means 6, because you subtract if the smaller number comes first. The following list goes in order, so you can figure out for yourself how to count to 44 in Roman numerals.

Super Bowls are numbered starting with Super Bowl I after the 1966 season. This is because the regular season lasts from September through December, but the championship game isn't played until the next year. The New Orleans Saints won the Super Bowl in 2010, but they were the champions of the season that was played in fall 2009.

**FUN FACT**

**MOST SUPER BOWL VICTORIES**

The Pittsburg Steelers have won 6 Super Bowls, more than any other team.

**I.** Packers 35, Chiefs 10. This was the first AFL-NFL championship game, but it wasn't yet called the Super Bowl.

**II.** Packers 33, Raiders 14. Packers coach Vince Lombardi won his last world championship.

**III.** Jets 16, (Baltimore) Colts 7. Joe Namath's Jets showed everyone that the AFL was just as good as the NFL.

**IV.** Chiefs 23, Vikings 7.

**V.** (Baltimore) Colts 16, Cowboys 13. Chuck Howley of the Cowboys was voted the game's most valuable player, even though his team lost.

**VI.** Cowboys 24, Dolphins 3.

**VII.** Dolphins 14, Redskins 7. The 1972 Dolphins became the first team in NFL history to complete an undefeated season.

**VIII.** Dolphins 24, Vikings 7. The Dolphins were the first team to appear in the Super Bowl 3 years in a row.

**IX.** Steelers 16, Vikings 6. The Vikings lost their third of 4 Super Bowls.

**X.** Steelers 21, Cowboys 17. The Steelers came from behind with 2 touchdowns in the fourth quarter, then intercepted a pass on the last play of the game.

**XI.** Raiders 32, Vikings 14. Raiders head coach and hall of famer John Madden won his only Super Bowl.

**XII.** Cowboys 27, Broncos 10.

**XIII.** Steelers 35, Cowboys 31. The Steelers won again in the matchup of the greatest teams of the 1970s.

**XIV** Steelers 31, (Los Angeles) Rams 19. The Steelers won their fourth Super Bowl in 4 tries.

**XV.** Raiders 27, Eagles 10.

**XVI.** 49ers 26, Bengals 21. San Francisco quarterback Joe Montana led his team to a 20-0 halftime lead. The San Francisco defense forced 5 turnovers.

**XVII.** Redskins 27, Dolphins 17. Washington quarterback Joe Theismann won his only Super Bowl.

**XVIII.** (Los Angeles) Raiders 38, Redskins 9. This would be the last victory for the AFC for 14 years.

**XIX.** 49ers 38, Dolphins 16. In his only Super Bowl appearance, Miami quarterback Dan Marino lost to Joe Montana's 49ers.

**XX.** Bears 46, Patriots 10. Coach Mike Ditka led his overwhelming favorite Bears to a convincing victory.

**XXI.** Giants 39, Broncos 20. Giants coach Bill Parcells won his first of 3 Super Bowl appearances.

**XXII.** Redskins 42, Broncos 10. Skins quarterback Doug Williams not only became the first black quarterback in the Super Bowl, but he was the game's MVP.

**XXIII.** 49ers 20, Bengals 16. Joe Montana threw the winning TD to John Taylor with 34 seconds remaining, but 49ers receiver Jerry Rice was the MVP.

**XXIV.** 49ers 55, Broncos 10. Ho-hum, Joe Montana won his fourth Super Bowl and his third MVP award.

## FUN FACT

### THE FIRST PROFESSIONAL FOOTBALL PLAYER

In 1892, the Allegheny Athletic Association paid Pudge Heffelfinger $500 to play in a game against the Pittsburgh Athletic Club. That amount of money is equivalent to about $10,000 today. That sounds like a lot, but even a rookie in today's NFL makes nearly $20,000 per game, and most players make a lot more.

**XXV.** Giants 20, Bills 19. Scott Norwood's 47-yard field goal attempt went wide right as time expired.

**XXVI.** Redskins 37, Bills 24.

**XXVII.** Cowboys 52, Bills 17. Dallas quarterback Troy Aikman won his first of 3 Super Bowls.

**XXVIII.** Cowboys 30, Bills 13. The Bills tied the Vikings and the Broncos with 4 Super Bowl appearances and 4 losses.

**XXIX.** 49ers 49, Chargers 26. This time the 49ers were led by quarterback Steve Young, who threw 6 touchdowns.

**XXX.** Cowboys 27, Steelers 17.

**XXXI.** Packers 35, Patriots 21. QB Brett Favre led a resurgence of the Packers franchise, which had not seen such good times since the days of coach Vince Lombardi.

**XXXII.** Broncos 31, Packers 24. Though the Broncos had 4 four previous Super Bowls, they won this time behind a tremendous rushing attack.

**XXXIII.** Broncos 34, Falcons 19. Quarterback John Elway won his second straight Super Bowl and the MVP trophy as well.

**XXXIV.** Rams 23, Titans 16. The Titans had one last play from the 10-yard line, but Mike Jones tackled receiver Kevin Dyson at the 1-yard line to seal the game.

**XXXV.** Ravens 34, Giants 7. The Ravens defense dominated this game, allowing only a special teams touchdown.

**XXXVI.** Patriots 20, Rams 17. Kicker Adam Vinatieri nailed a 48-yard field goal to end the game. First-year starting quarterback Tom Brady was MVP.

**XXXVII.** Buccaneers 48, Raiders 21. The Tampa defense intercepted quarterback Rich Gannon 5 times, returning 3 for touchdowns.

**XXXVIII.** Patriots 32, Panthers 29. Once again Adam Vinatieri won the game with a last-second field goal, and once again quarterback Tom Brady was the MVP.

**xxxix.** Patriots 24, Eagles 21. Vinatieri, Brady, and coach Bill Belichick won another close game.

**xl.** Steelers 21, Seahawks 10. Receiver Hines Ward and running back Jerome Bettis were the offensive heroes of the Steelers, who had just barely made the playoffs.

**xli.** Colts 29, Bears 17. Peyton Manning, who had been a top-rated quarterback for 7 years without a championship, showed he could come through in a big game.

**xlii.** Giants 17, Patriots 14. David Tyree's famous "helmet catch" helped defeat New England, who had not lost a game all year until the Super Bowl.

# Find the Football

Find the one time that FOOTBALL is spelled correctly. Look up and down, side-to-side, and backwards!

```
T A B O O L O F
F O O T T O B A O L O O
B F O O F O F O O T T B A L L
T A O L F L O O F O O B L A L F
F O O T B F O O O T B A L A L O O F
F O O T O L T A O B B O L F L F L O A B
F O O B T L L A B T O O F B O F T O
B A A O F O O T T O F B A L F O
F L O T B A F O L O F O T O
L F O O T A O A O L L O
T O O L B A T O
```

**XLIII.** Steelers 27, Cardinals 23. The game ended with an amazing touchdown pass to MVP Santonio Holmes in the back corner of the end zone.

**XLIV.** Saints 31, Colts 17. Saints quarterback and MVP Drew Brees led a come-from-behind victory against the favored Colts.

**XLV.** Packers 31, Steelers 25. The Packers were the sixth Wild Card team to win a Super Bowl, and the third team to do so after winning 3 road playoff games.

Super Bowl XLV in 2011 was the most watched Super Bowl ever; an average of 111 million people were tuned into the game at any given moment. The only sporting event in the world that is more significant is soccer's World Cup.

## Soccer

The World Cup is an international soccer competition that is held every 4 years. In the United States, the Super Bowl and the World Series are bigger events, but worldwide, the World Cup is the number one sporting competition. Roughly 200 countries compete to be the top soccer team in the world.

As you can imagine, planning the World Cup is a pretty big deal! Trying to narrow down 200 countries into 1 final winner takes a lot of time and involves tons of matches. The years in between each World Cup are spent qualifying for the next one. Only 32 of those original 200 countries get to go.

So who are the lucky ones? Well, first of all, the country who hosts the World Cup automatically gets in, so countries are very eager to be the hosts. The Fédération Internationale de Football Association (FIFA) moves the Cup all over the world to make it fair, but not every country is able to provide the sta-

**DID YOU KNOW?** ⋯⋯⋯

A single soccer player runs about 7 miles per game.

# FUN FACT

### JUST A KID

At the age of 14, Freddy Adu became the youngest person to ever play for a professional sports team in the United States. He was signed by the DC United. Not surprisingly, he also became the youngest person to ever score a goal for Major League Soccer, which he also did at age 14.

diums and handle the crowds. Germany hosted in 2006, South Africa in 2010, and Brazil will host in 2014.

So, the host team is 1 team of the 32. Then the defending champions from the previous World Cup automatically get in. That's 2. The rest of the teams have to earn 1 of the remaining 30 spots by playing qualifying matches.

FIFA divides the world into 10 divisions. Then each team in that division plays qualifying matches against the other teams in that division. When the matches are all done, the top 3 teams in each division qualify for the World Cup, making up the 30 remaining spots for the competition.

Then the World Cup begins. The teams are divided into 8 groups with 4 teams each. FIFA looks at the scores and the win/loss records of all the qualifying matches and then spreads the top teams throughout the 8 groups, so they aren't all playing each other in the first round.

Finally it's summer, and it's time for the World Cup competition to begin. The first round of the tournament is played as a round robin. Each team plays the other 3 teams in the group. The 2 teams that come out of that little competition with the best record move on. So, do the math. How many are eliminated and how many move on? If you guess 16 for both, you're right!

Now it's single elimination time. The winner of group A plays the runner-up of group B. The winner of group B plays the runner-up of group A. The winner of group C plays the runner-up of group D, and so on. The teams play one game,

# Keep Your Eye on the Ball

All thirteen of the words in this puzzle can be followed by the word BALL. See how many words you can figure out and fit into the criss-cross grid. HINT: We've left you the first letter of each!

| | | |
|---|---|---|
| Soccer | Wiffle | Basket |
| Base | Ping pong | Snow |
| Foot | Tee | Bowling |
| Golf | Tether | |
| Tennis | Dodge | |

## FUN FACT

### THE GOAL OF THE CENTURY

In 2002, FIFA asked fans to vote for their favorite goal of the twentieth century. The winner was a goal made by Argentina's Diego Maradona in the 1986 World Cup tournament. He received the ball on his team's side of the field and then managed to dribble 60 meters, through five different defenders, take the shot, and score.

## DID YOU KNOW? ........

More than 80 percent of the world's soccer balls are produced in Pakistan.

## DID YOU KNOW? ........

India pulled out of the 1950 World Cup because the players were not allowed to play without shoes.

and the winners of that game move on. Now we're down to 8 teams, and it's single elimination the rest of the way until there's a single final winner.

Here are the winning countries since the World Cup began in 1930:

- 1930: Uruguay
- 1934: Italy
- 1938: Italy
- 1942: No World Cup because of World War II
- 1946: No World Cup because of World War II
- 1950: Uruguay
- 1954: West Germany
- 1958: Brazil
- 1962: Brazil
- 1966: England
- 1970: Brazil
- 1974: West Germany
- 1982: Italy
- 1986: Argentina
- 1990: Germany
- 1994: Brazil
- 1998: France
- 2002: Brazil
- 2006: Italy
- 2010: Spain

The Women's World Cup began in 1991, so it is much newer. Also, participation in women's sports is still growing around the world, so there aren't as many countries competing. In 1991 and 1995, there were only 12 countries participating. In 1999, however, it jumped to 16 teams, and the fan base has been growing every year.

Here are the winning countries for the Women's World Cup:

- 1991: United States
- 1995: Norway
- 1999: United States
- 2003: Germany
- 2007: Germany

The 2011 Women's World Cup will be played in Germany.

# CHAPTER 5
# Dangerous Dinosaurs

Chances are, you've seen a lot of different types of animals. But have you ever seen a dinosaur, even in a zoo? Of course not. The only dinosaurs we see today are in books, movies, or toy stores. So how do we know that the dinosaurs were ever really here? The only proof we have is in the form of fossilized bones or skeletons of these reptiles.

## The First Discovery

What would you think if you had never heard of a dinosaur and you found an enormous bone in your backyard? Not long after America was settled, a man found what he thought was part of a giant human. In fact, it turned out to be a bone from the meat-eater Megalosaurus!

This bone was the first of its kind to be named *dinosaur*, which means "great lizard." For centuries, any dinosaur that looked like it could have or would have eaten meat was called a *Megalosaurus*. This type of dinosaur would never have had to go to the dentist, because it always had new teeth waiting to replace any teeth that were lost or harmed.

After Megalosaurus, the next dinosaur to be given a scientific name was Iguanodon, which means "iguana tooth." Imagine sifting through a pile of rocks and finding a giant tooth! This happened one day to Dr. Gideon Mantell's wife, Mary Ann. It was found in the southern part of England, which remains a prime hunting ground for dinosaur fossils to this day.

When Mary Ann showed her discovery to her husband, he thought that it resembled a modern-day iguana's tooth. He also discovered another chunk of a fossil with a sharp spike that he believed was part of the dinosaur's nose. Thirty skeletons similar to the Iguanodon's then were found in a coal mine in Belgium, and scientists could tell from looking at them that the spike Dr. Mantell thought was a nose was actually more like a thumb.

**DID YOU KNOW?** ·········

The movie *Jurassic Park* depicts a Velociraptor adapting to a modern environment, learning how to turn and open door handles, and outsmarting humans. Yet in reality the Velociraptor would have been no smarter than a chicken.

## FUN FACT

### BILLIONS OF YEARS

Scientists believe that the earth is more than 4 billion years old. The dinosaur bones that have been found on earth are believed to be only millions of years old.

# Ptiny Pterosaurs

Some of the smallest pterosaurs were so lightweight that they had to be careful to keep their wings folded when they were resting. Otherwise, the wind could blow them right off their perch! Can you help this pterosaur catch a dragonfly for dinner?

## FUN FACT

### SOMETHING'S MISSING!

No matter how hard the dinosaur hunters have tried, no one has been able to find a complete Tyrannosaurus rex skeleton. They have found enough bones to give us a good idea of what T. rex was like, but they were not all found in the same place.

## FUN FACT

### EVIDENCE OF A MEAL

One way that scientists know that some of the dinosaurs ate other dinosaurs is that their fossils show the remains of these other dinosaurs still in the stomach of the dinosaurs that ate them!

Before this mistake had been straightened out, a sculpture, bearing the horn or spike-like nose, had been created in Crystal Park in London. This life-size model is large enough to hold more than 20 people at a time, and is still on display today.

## Ferocious Fighters

When the carnosaurs, or "flesh lizards," appeared on the scene in the Jurassic times, there was no question about who was the king of that jungle. One of these carnosaurs, Allosaurus, was the size of a large bus, weighed as much as a rhinoceros, and had teeth about 4 inches long!

How would you like to live in the same world with this dinosaur? Scientists also think the Allosaurus hunted in groups or packs. There would be no doubt who would win when it came to the larger and more ferocious dinosaurs like this one.

Two other dinosaurs, known as Ceratosaurus and Megalosaurus, were only half as big as Allosaurus, but they probably could have ambushed larger dinosaurs and earned the title of winners if they wanted to. But usually, if they were unsuccessful at their hunting, they acted more like buzzards, which are the garbage collectors of our modern world, and ate whatever scraps or remains were left lying around. These reptiles were so strong, scientists came up with a new name for them—they called them *archosaurs*.

## Camouflaged Cover

One of the ways a dinosaur could fight for its life would be to run for cover. From some of the fossils that have been found, we can see that like many of today's lizards and snakes, certain dinosaurs may have been camouflaged, making them almost invisible in certain hiding places.

# Full Plates

Break the letter-shifting code by writing the letters either one before or one after the letters shown on each of the Stegosaurus's plates.

When you have written in the correct letters, you will have the answer to the riddle.

*What do you call a dinosaur who makes noise as he sleeps?*

F N R M
D N
S N
Q T
R R
S

If you were going out to play hide and seek and you wanted to camouflage yourself so you could hide better by blending in with the background, you could have an adult help you use different colored face paints and clothing to match the setting. Use black for night, brown for mud, green for the grass or trees, and tan for the sand and beach.

## Giant Food Problems

Did the sauropod dinosaurs become extinct because they had weak or bad teeth that were only good for scraping off leaves? Many sauropod fossil skeletons have been found with stones known as *gastroliths* in their stomach area. They were only able to digest their food by swallowing these "stomach stones," which helped grind up the food in their stomachs. Today, chickens have a digestive organ called a *gizzard* that's filled with tiny stones to grind up their food.

## FUN FACT

### TWO BRAINS?

For many years, scientists believed that the Brachiosaurus was so large that it needed a second brain. They thought this second brain was located above its hips and that it might have helped the dinosaur to move its legs. Then they decided that what they had found was not another brain, but just a large bump on its spinal cord.

## FUN FACT

### A DINO-TRUNK?

The Brachiosaurus had holes for nostrils in its forehead above its eyes. For many years, some scientists believed that these dinosaurs went under the water to eat and breathed through the nostril holes, which would have been just above the surface of the water. Scientists no longer believe that dinosaurs could survive with their bodies under that much water pressure, so now they are wondering if maybe there was a trunk fastened to these holes! Elephants have holes in almost the same spot on their heads.

### DID YOU KNOW? ........

There were no flying or swimming dinosaurs. The swimming "dinosaurs" that are often depicted were really aquatic reptiles.

Scientists think that the plant-eaters spent most of each day collecting their food, and some of them needed up to 300 pounds of food each day to survive! This need for so much food leaves the scientists wondering how any animal with such a small head on such a huge body could ever gather enough to eat!

## Miniature Monsters

If you could see a picture of Compsognathus, the dinosaur known as "pretty jaw," you might wonder if the fossil hunter who named it had a very vivid imagination. Its head was more delicate than most of the other meat-eaters and you couldn't see its sharp teeth, but it definitely was a killer. It also had a delicate body, weighing as little as a large chicken, but it was as tall as a young human teenager.

The geckoes or chameleons that you can find in a pet store look a lot like a very small version of this dinosaur. Some fossil hunters in Germany once thought that they had found another Compsognathus fossil, until they discovered that it had wings, feathers, and feet that could perch on a tree branch! It turned out they had discovered a new dinosaur called Archaeopteryx. Even though the Archaeopteryx had wings and feathers it wasn't actually a bird, but it wasn't really a reptile either, because it also had teeth, claws on its wings, and a long tail like a snake! Some scientists think that Archaeopteryx was the first bird descended from dinosaurs.

There were not very many small meat-eating dinosaurs in the Jurassic Period. Ornitholestes, who was one of them, only weighed as much as a medium-sized dog, but its long, curved claws and sharp teeth made it easy for Ornitholestes to eat its food. It was nicknamed the "bird robber," because some fossil hunters believed its diet consisted of early birds like

Archaeopteryx. However, none of the Ornitholestes and Archaeopteryx fossils have been found in the same place, so now this is no longer believed to be true.

## Plated Puzzles

The plated dinosaurs were some of the last and most unusual varieties of dinosaurs to appear in the Jurassic period. The bodies of Scelidosaurus and Scutellosaurus were covered with small plates like a sort of flexible armor. Scientists think that these dinosaurs could have been the ancestors of either the Stegosaurus or the Anklyosaurus.

You might be mad if someone called you a birdbrain, but you should be more upset if they called you a Stegosaurus-brain. Why? Because a Stegosaurus's body was larger than the biggest van, yet its brain was probably only the size of a walnut. Scientists used to think that the Stegosaurus, like the Brachiosaurus, had a second brain located in the area above its hips that helped control its legs, but they found out that wasn't true. Almost everything about the Stegosaurus was different from other dinosaurs, including its tail, which was longer than the rest of its body and covered with long spikes at the end. Its name, "roofed lizard," comes from the huge plates that scientists first believed covered its back like tiles on a roof. Because its bones were in a pile when paleontologists found them, scientists aren't sure how

# Keep Looking

Can you find the one and only time in the letter grid that the word FOSSIL is spelled correctly? The answer might be side to side, top to bottom, diagonal, or backward! Use a marker to color in the boxes where the word FOSSIL is found.

| Q | O | Q | Q | T | P | K | I | E |
| T | K | S | E | E | P | S | E | Q |
| K | T | Q | S | K | S | T | Q | P |
| E | Q | P | K | O | T | K | P | P |
| T | Q | K | L | F | O | E | Q | E |
| I | L | F | O | S | L | L | I | L |
| Q | E | P | O | O | I | K | T | T |
| F | F | O | S | S | I | L | O |
| P | E | Q | F | S | S | T | Q | Q |
| F | O | S | S | I | O | F | O | S |
| Q | E | P | I | L | F | P | Q | E |
| L | I | S | S | F | O | S | S | I |
| E | Q | P | S | O | S | E | Q | P |
| O | S | F | O | S | S | L | I | F |
| T | D | Q | F | S | I | K | T | Q |
| E | Q | P | T | I | K | Q | K | K |

**EXTRA FUN:** Use the same marker to fill in ALL the boxes where the letters F-O-S-S-I-L are found. What have you uncovered?

# Why Did the Dinosaur Cross the Road?

Find the correct path for this dinosaur from START to END. Pick up letters along the way that will spell the answer to this riddle.

START

END

the plates were arranged. They also wonder if the plates were colored like a rainbow to attract or frighten other dinosaurs, or if they were used like solar panels to warm up the Stegosaurus on cold mornings.

Stegosaurus's cousin, the Kentrosaurus, whose fossils were found in Germany, had many more spikes than did Stegosaurus. The Kentrosaurus's spikes seem to have run all the way from the tip of its tail to the top of its hips, rather than being only at the end of the tail like the Stegosaurus.

## Footprints: Why Do They Make Them This Way?

You probably haven't thought much about different types of shoes or the prints or impressions that they make. If you have thought about them, probably all you were interested in is how they look. Have you ever looked at the soles of your shoes and wondered why they are made the way that they are? Were the designers trying to duplicate the bottom of an animal's foot so you could get better traction for climbing hills or to be able to run fast or stop quickly?

You could try playing a game of shoe-track hide-and-seek. To start, all you need are a few friends who are wearing pairs of old shoes. The object of the game is to follow the prints, so you will want to play in the sand or dirt where you can see tracks. (This also would be a great game to play in the winter, just after a fresh snowfall! Except in that case, make sure to wear boots!) Everyone should take turns looking at the soles of each other's shoes or boots. Next, if you're the seeker, close your eyes and count to 100 while everyone else hides, and then start following the tracks.

When you get close to the person who is hiding, stop and try to guess who it is by the shoe print. If you're right, that person becomes the next seeker. Do you think the dinosaurs

**FUN FACT**

**WHAT COLOR WAS THAT DINOSAUR?**

Although the skins of several fossilized dinosaurs show different textures and patterns, the color of their skin is a mystery. The colors of the dinosaurs we see in pictures or movies today are only guesses of what their true color may have been.

followed each other's tracks? Or do you think they found each other in different ways?

### Feet Facts

When the dinosaurs were discovered, scientists divided them into classes by the type of hips and feet that they had. Plateosaurus was called a *prosauropod,* which means "before lizard feet"; it was considered by some scientists to be the link between the "beast-feet" theropods (like Megalosaurus) and the "lizard-feet" sauropods (like Apatosaurus).

All of these dinosaurs came before the "bird-feet" ornithopods (like Iguanodon). To make it even more confusing, prosauropods, theropods, and sauropods were all classed as "lizard-hipped" saurischians, and ornithopods were classed as "bird-hipped" ornithischians.

Whether they are labeled as beast, lizard, or bird feet, you would probably have to be a scientist to see much difference between these dinosaurs' tracks, other than the fact that the number of fingers and toes kept changing over the years and some of the claws changed into hooves.

### Real Dinosaur Tracks?

In one place there are preserved dinosaur tracks that look as though the dinosaurs walked straight up a rock wall. This illusion was created when mountains rose, pushing a slab of stone that had once been part of a riverbed up into the air.

The real mystery is how the prints managed to remain there through all these years when they were made in soft mud. Normally, rain should have washed them away, unless there wasn't any more rain for a very long time.

If you would like to know more about visiting other places to see dinosaur fossils and prints, you can visit your library or

### HOME SWEET BONE

There were so many dinosaur bones found in one place in Wyoming that a shepherd built a cabin out of them. The place eventually became known as Bone Cabin Quarry!

go on your Internet search page and type in "dinosaur tracks" in your search box.

### Tracking Them Down

Did you know that real-life detectives make plaster casts of footprints and tire tracks from a crime scene and then use them for evidence? They can use the casts to try to find out who has shoes or tires like the tracks that they found. You can try this, too! To make a cast of a track, first ask an adult to help you gather the following items.

### Materials

- A disposable cup
- A plastic bag
- Dry plaster of Paris
- A container of water
- A pair of disposable gloves

### Procedure

1. Find a track in the ground.
2. Pour your plaster of Paris in the cup.
3. Add enough water to make it like mud.
4. Stir it until it is mixed completely.
5. Pour it over the track and let it dry. When the plaster is dry, you can lift it up out of the ground and you will have a cast of the print.

## Do You Believe in Giants?

When you look at your parents, they probably seem pretty tall to you, but can you imagine living in the same world with

## DID YOU KNOW? ·········

Some dinosaurs took care of their babies, but not all did. Some just laid their eggs and left. They didn't do this to be mean, though; it was really to help the babies survive. In some cases the mother dinosaur was so big she would have accidentally crushed her own babies just by moving around.

an animal that was so big that just one vertebra, which was one of the many pieces of its backbone, was as tall as an adult human? That dinosaur was called *Seismosaurus*, because he weighed so much that people think each step he took probably made the earth quake!

Scientists can measure and record the vibrations that come from an earthquake by using machines called *seismographs*. Do you think they would use them to warn us when the dinosaurs were coming near if the "great lizards" were still living today? Just imagine if you heard something that weighed twice as much as a semitrailer coming down a trail after you! Look out!!!!!

## What about Giant People?

We know there were giant dinosaurs, because we have found their fossils, but can we prove whether giant men or women ever roamed the earth? There have been many stories about big men both in fairy tales and recorded throughout history. Maybe you've heard stories about the logger Paul Bunyan with Babe, his famous blue ox. Or maybe you've heard the tale about the giant that Jack killed after climbing the beanstalk, or the Bible story about David slaying the enormous Goliath.

Many of today's basketball players are certainly a lot bigger than the average adult is. A century ago, very few men were 6 feet tall, but now there are a lot of them. In the past, when people grew more than 7 feet tall, it was usually due to something that was wrong with a gland in their necks called the *pituitary gland*. The pituitary gland has many purposes, but most people think of it as a "growth gland."

Do you think that some of the dinosaurs had something wrong with their pituitary gland, or do you think they grew so big because of something that they ate? If you could eat something that would make you a lot bigger, would you want to? Just for fun, you could get out your measuring tape and see how tall your friends and family are. Some people say that if you take the height you were when you were two years old and then you multiply that measurement times two, you will come up with the height you will be when you grow up. Maybe the dinosaurs doubled their size, too!

## An Appetite to Match Their Size

Have you ever been to the top of a six-story building? Sauroposeidon, named after Poseidon, the god of the sea, would have been able to look right into the top windows of that building! Some people think that Sauroposeidon ate leaves by swinging his neck around in a circle, because it would have been too much work to move his large body all of the time. This way, he could eat everything within his reach before moving on to the next bunch of trees.

If you were that big, it would probably take a truckload of hamburgers and hot dogs to fill you up. When the dinosaurs ate all of the tree leaves in their neighborhood, they had to keep moving to new sources of food or they would starve. Scientists believe that dinosaur herds traveled long distances in search of food.

You might be thinking that with such a great need for food it wasn't the best thing to be as big as a Sauroposeidon, but there were some advantages. Who would argue with an animal that could crush someone just by leaning on him, or that could send someone flying like a soccer ball with one flick of its massive tail? Once the sun warmed the dinosaur's huge body during the day, it would stay warm all through the night! There wouldn't have been any need for a giant blanket.

**DID YOU KNOW?** • • • • • • • • •

Did you know dinosaurs could use bad breath as a weapon? Its true, paleontologists believe that some dinosaurs like the Tyrannosaurus had teeth that were made to hold on to dead tissue. After a while the dead tissue would rot and breed harmful bacteria and monstrous bad breath. If the Tyrannosaurus bit another dinosaur, the bacteria would cause an infectious wound that would cause the bitten dinosaur to die. Then the Tyrannosaurus could come back and collect its meal.

## What about Dragons?

Have your parents read any fairy tales to you? Many fairy tales describe creatures that looked like flying dragons. For thousands of years, children all over the world have heard stories about dragons.

Dinosaur hunters have found many dinosaur fossils in the same lands where the stories are told, and some of the dinosaurs certainly did look like dragons without wings.

A pterosaur fossil looks a lot like a dragon because of its long tail, big teeth, and the claws on its wings! You could almost imagine it breathing fire! Or maybe there was no fire, but just a cloud from the pterosaur's mouth that came from its warm breath in the cold air. Have you ever seen your breath on a cold day?

Most people did not believe that the dragon-like dinosaurs really existed until they started finding their big bones in England during the 1800s. The dinosaur Spinosaurus also looked like a dragon with its long jaws and the huge wing-type "sail" on its back. Scientists believe that several of the dinosaurs, including Ouranosaurus, Rebbachisaurus, and Amargasaurus, had this same type of sail. They also believe that the "sail" on the reptile Dimetrodon was similar to the dinosaurs' sail, and that this was a type of heat regulator for all of them. If they became too hot, they turned their backs to the sun. If they became too cold, they turned their sides toward the sun to let their "sails" absorb all that heat.

# CHAPTER 6
# Nonsense Nature

Have you ever heard of "Mother Nature"? The term *nature* includes our world and the many things that live there. Sometimes, that means exotic life in faraway places, like poison dart frogs in a rainforest in South America. But nature is also as close as your backyard or the neighborhood park.

Can you even find nature in a crowded city? Definitely! Trees line city streets or grow in parks. Pigeons and other birds flutter about. Even pesky insects and other critters are part of nature in the city. (We just want them to stay out of our homes!)

Our world is incredibly large, and so is the world of nature. Discovering nature is a life-long experience. Try to find some today!

## Our World: Just Right for Life

Remember when we said that conditions for life on Earth are just right? We have just the right temperature and plenty of water for living things to grow. Did you know that about 90 percent of your own body is water? How about that!

Earth also has the right atmosphere for life. As nature writer Rachel Carson put it, we live in an "ocean of air." It ranges from the Earth's surface upward toward space.

By volume, air is about 77 percent nitrogen and 21 percent oxygen. We and many other animals need oxygen to breathe. Other chemicals in the air are argon, carbon dioxide, hydrogen, neon, helium, krypton, and xenon. Water vapor—evaporated water—is also in the air.

The atmosphere acts like a blanket. It captures just enough of the sun's warmth and holds it in. Without the atmosphere, Earth's sunny side would be way too hot, and its dark side would be bitterly cold. (Remember, that's what happens on the moon!)

### DID YOU KNOW? ........

We have explored less than 5 percent of our planet's oceans. In fact we have better drawings and maps of Mars than we do of our own oceans' floors.

The atmosphere is also a sunscreen. You know how you can wear a hat and sunglasses in the summer to protect your skin and your eyes? Well, the earth's ozone layer also screens out many of the sun's harmful ultraviolet rays. Our distance from the sun and the presence of water and atmosphere are all just right on Earth. They help life thrive on our planet.

## Making Mountains

Scientists believe Earth was formed 4.5 billion years ago. Earth's inner core is solid rock. Surrounding it is an outer core of molten, or melted, rock.

Around the core is the mantle layer. Above the mantle lies Earth's crust. Beneath some parts of the ocean, the crust is only about five miles deep. Under some mountain ranges, however, it's 50 miles (80 km) deep.

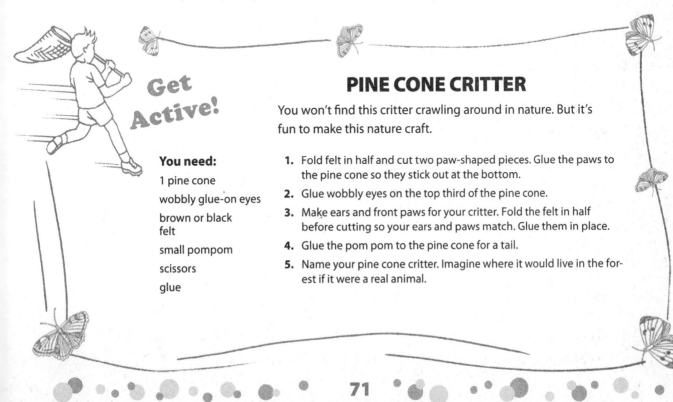

*Get Active!*

## PINE CONE CRITTER

You won't find this critter crawling around in nature. But it's fun to make this nature craft.

**You need:**

1 pine cone

wobbly glue-on eyes

brown or black felt

small pompom

scissors

glue

1. Fold felt in half and cut two paw-shaped pieces. Glue the paws to the pine cone so they stick out at the bottom.
2. Glue wobbly eyes on the top third of the pine cone.
3. Make ears and front paws for your critter. Fold the felt in half before cutting so your ears and paws match. Glue them in place.
4. Glue the pom pom to the pine cone for a tail.
5. Name your pine cone critter. Imagine where it would live in the forest if it were a real animal.

## DID YOU KNOW? ·········

Approximately 4,000 people have tried to climb Mount Everest. Of those, only 660 people have successfully made it to the top. To date 142 people have died while trying to climb the mountain.

The crust is divided into fifteen areas, called *tectonic plates*. Rising above the oceans on the plates are the seven continents: Asia, Africa, North America, South America, Europe, Australia, and Antarctica.

The plates "float" on top of the mantle. A long time ago, when Earth's plates collided, they pushed the ground up, forming majestic mountains.

The Himalayas in Nepal, India, and China are Earth's tallest mountains. They began forming over 30 million years ago. Mount Everest is the highest peak at 29,030 feet (8,850 m)—over five miles high!

The Rocky Mountains, Alps, Appalachians, Andes, and Ural Mountains also formed from plate movement. When you see a mountain scene, think about how long it took to create each magnificent peak. The mountains were formed when two of the Earth's tectonic plates slammed into each other.

## Get Active!

### TECTONIC PASTA

**NOTE:** Use caution with all kitchen appliances. Get adult supervision while using the stove.

**You need:**

2 uncooked lasagna noodles

wide pot with water

1. Break the noodles into 12 pieces. Imagine that your noodles are continents sitting on tectonic plates, and that the water is Earth's mantle of molten rock.

2. Float the pieces on top of the water. Bump them against each other to demonstrate mountain building. Make them move away from each other to show continental spread. Rub them against each other to mimic an earthquake.

3. Put the noodles on a plate. Boil the water. Then carefully put the noodles back in the pot. Lower the heat slightly so the water won't boil over.

4. Pressure from heat currents makes the water bubble up. Inside the earth, pressure from heat currents makes volcanoes erupt. Heat currents make the boiling water move the noodles around.

5. After about 14 minutes, turn off the heat. Remove the noodles with a slotted spoon. Add butter and parsley. Then enjoy your tectonic pasta.

What happens when you slide your foot into the edge of a rug? Your foot pushes the rug, and the material scrunches together. This is similar to what happens when two tectonic plates run into each other—only it takes much longer to form a whole mountain!

## Natural Disaster: Volcanoes

Volcanoes look like mountains. But instead of being pushed up gradually, volcanoes form when part of the material inside the earth gets out. Earth's core is very hot—about 4,500 degrees Celsius (°C). Heat causes molten rock to rise. The molten rock needs somewhere to go.

Volcanoes erupt when mounting pressure breaks through the Earth's crust. In the most violent eruptions, huge black clouds of lava, ash, and dust spit out from the top. Molten lava races along the ground, burning everything in its path. Volcanic eruptions can also trigger earthquakes and giant waves, which are called *tsunamis*.

Volcanoes build up land surface, but eruptions can also be deadly. Mount Soufriere's eruptions during the 1990s destroyed most homes on the Caribbean island of Montserrat. A 1985 volcanic eruption killed 23,000 people in Colombia. The Krakatoa eruption in Indonesia in 1883 killed over 36,000 people.

## Natural Disaster: Earthquakes

Just as the World Series game was to start on October 17, 1989, people at San Francisco's Candlestick Park felt a rumbling. It was an earthquake along California's San Andreas fault. The earthquake killed 67 people in the San Francisco Bay area.

## FUN FACT

### HAWAIIAN ISLANDS

The Hawaiian Islands were built by volcanic action on the floor of the Pacific Ocean. Some of the islands' volcanoes are still active. The Kilauea volcano, one of the world's most active volcanoes, erupted in March 2011 shooting lava 65 feet high!

## FUN FACT

### THE TOHOKU EARTHQUAKE

The earthquake that struck Japan in March 2011 was a level 9. It was the most powerful earthquake to ever strike Japan and the fifth most powerful in the world. The earthquake also triggered destructive tsunami waves of up to 128 feet that struck Japan.

## FUN FACT

### MAKE YOUR OWN WAVELENGTH

You and a friend can demonstrate wavelengths by holding two ends of a rope. Move one end slowly from side to side for long wavelengths. Wiggle it quickly for shorter wavelengths.

Earthquakes occur most often near edges of tectonic plates. The edges are called *fault lines*. Plates slipping or scraping against each other release energy inside the Earth.

Earthquakes may last only a minute, but they can do tremendous damage. Thousands of people died in 1999 after major earthquakes struck Turkey, Greece, and Taiwan. Scientists measure earthquakes with two scales. The Richter scale gauges how much energy was released at the earthquake's source. Each whole number on the Richter scale is a tenfold increase over the previous number. Level 2 is barely detectable. Level 6 is moderately destructive. Level 8 is total damage.

The modified Mercalli scale ranges from I through XII. It describes how an earthquake is felt at a specific place. Level I earthquakes are barely felt. Level VI earthquakes are felt by everyone.

## Natural Phenomena: Sunrise and Sunset

What causes sunrise and sunset? As we discussed earlier, although the sun seems to move, it's really Earth that's moving. Earth always spins, or rotates, toward the east. Unless clouds block the sun, the sky usually looks blue. In fact, however, sunlight contains all colors of light. Red, orange, yellow, green, blue, indigo, and violet make up the visible spectrum of light. Put them all together, and you get white, which is why sunlight looks white.

Different colors of light have different wavelengths. A wavelength is the distance between one wave crest, or top, and the next one. Violet, indigo, and blue have the shortest wavelengths. Red, orange, and yellow have longer wavelengths.

As light waves enter the atmosphere, they strike gas and particle molecules in the air. The molecules scatter the light. That is, they split the different colors apart. This phenomenon is called *Rayleigh scattering*.

The shorter bluish wavelengths get scattered about four times more easily than the longer reddish wavelengths. Because they reach our eyes from all directions in the sky, the sky looks blue.

Near sunrise and sunset, however, the sun's rays must travel through more of the atmosphere to reach us. By then, most bluish wavelengths are scattered away. The longer red wavelengths make the sky glow orange or red.

## What Makes the Colors in the Rainbow?

If you have a prism, you can separate sunlight into its individual colors. A typical prism looks like a triangular column of glass. As light passes through, the glass bends the light. The bending lets you see the visible spectrum: red, orange, yellow, green, blue, indigo, and violet.

Rainbows result from nature's prisms. Sometimes after it stops raining overhead, droplets stay in the air ahead of you. If sun shines from behind you through the droplets, the drops act like prisms.

But light's reddish wavelengths are longer than the bluish wavelengths. They arch over the shorter wavelengths. This makes the rainbow curve.

Don't search for a pot of gold at the end of the rainbow! As you move, the projection of the rainbow moves too. When the air dries, the rainbow disappears.

## Changing Seasons

Do you have a favorite season? Spring's budding leaves, bright flowers, and warmer days bring new life. It's a great time to play outdoors, plant a garden, or watch a baseball game.

### FUN FACT

**THE GREEN FLASH**

Does the sky ever look green? Yes, but very rarely. The green flash sometimes happens literally "in a flash." Just before sunrise or just after sunset, light's reddish rays may be hidden below the horizon, while the blue hues get scattered by the air. That leaves the green rays, whose wavelengths lie between red and blue. We usually don't see the green flash. Dust and pollution can hide the flash. Trees, buildings, and anything else on the horizon can also hide it.

## DID YOU KNOW? . . . . . . . .

An ear of corn always has an even number of rows because of the division of its cells. In fact most things in nature have even rows, for example, a watermelon has an even number of stripes.

Hot summer days are great for swimming or playing at the beach. Sometimes a thunderstorm brings welcome relief from the heat.

Autumn days are crisp and cool. Tree leaves change to yellow, orange, red, and brown. Days get shorter.

The sun sets early in winter. Sledding, skating, and building snowmen are great fun on a cold winter day.

But wait! Not everyone experiences the seasons this way. While brisk December winds sweep across North Dakota, Los Angeles often gets warm, sunny days with temperatures over 75 degrees Fahrenheit. As New Englanders swelter from summer heat, Alaska can still have temperatures close to freezing.

Strangely enough, Earth is nearest the sun around January 3. Yet at that time, areas in the Northern Hemisphere have winter. Why? If you shine a flashlight directly at a wall, you'll see a bright spot. Angle it, and you'll cover a broader area with a dimmer beam.

The same thing happens with Earth. As Earth orbits the sun, its axis stays tilted. During summer, the sun's rays strike the Northern Hemisphere directly. It receives more light and heat.

Also during summer, the tilt brings more areas within the sun's range. Thus, summer days are longer and brighter.

In winter, the Northern Hemisphere tilts away from the sun. Light falls indirectly, at an angle. Temperatures fall as days get shorter.

What happens in the Southern Hemisphere? Because of Earth's tilt, seasons there are reversed. December brings the start of summer to Australia. Winter starts in June.

Even in summer, it's cooler in Alaska than it is in Florida. Distance from the equator makes the difference. Polar regions always get the sun's rays at a slant, so they stay cold year round! In contrast, direct sunlight brings more light and heat to areas near the equator. That means warmer weather all year round.

Prevailing winds, altitude (which means the land height above sea level), nearness to lakes or oceans, and other factors also affect an area's weather. One tropical area may be a rain forest, while another is a desert.

## Global Warming

Global warming may not seem like a bad idea when you're shivering on a winter day. But scientists warn that if Earth's temperature keeps warming up each year, even by just a little, eventually, it could be a real disaster.

The problem starts with too much carbon dioxide and other gases in the air. These gases come from driving cars, burning fuel, and many other activities. Cutting down forests—or even just burning parts of them—also releases gases to the air.

Over time, these gases can produce what is called a *greenhouse effect*. Have you ever seen a greenhouse? It's a warm place where people grow plants. The glass of a greenhouse traps the sun's heat inside, so that it's much warmer than the air outside—just like a car gets hot when the windows are closed on a sunny day.

In the same way, scientists say greenhouse gases trap more of the sun's heat in the atmosphere. Natural events, such as volcanic eruptions, can also cause temporary warming until clouds of volcanic ash settle.

By the year 2100, global temperatures could rise up to 6°F (3.5°C). Some of the rise may be natural, but some is likely due to people's activities.

Scientists worry that even that such a small rise could cause catastrophes. Hurricanes, typhoons, droughts, and other weather disasters could become much more severe. And, some of the polar ice could melt! That would lead to massive flooding.

Scientists concerned about global warming urge people to reduce greenhouse gases and stop cutting down forest areas. That way, they say, less carbon dioxide will build up in the atmosphere.

### Fight Greenhouse Gases

Here are five simple things you can do to reduce greenhouse gases.

1. Walk places with your friends and family instead of driving all the time.
2. Too far to walk? Take your bike! Or try public transportation. When everyone shares one bus or train, a lot less gas is produced than when everyone takes their own cars.
3. When you do travel by car, share rides with friends. Your parents will save driving time too.
4. Recycle materials at home. You'll save money and if we don't need as many new things, then factories won't use so much energy to make them!
5. Turn off lights when you leave a room. Less fuel gets burned that way.

## Energy from Nature

If you knew how much energy it took to make things, would you try to use less stuff? You might be surprised to learn the high cost in energy of the things you use every day. These esti-

**DID YOU KNOW?**

Oak trees do not grow acorns until they are at least 50 years old.

## Get Active!

## GO METEOR WATCHING

Want to see our atmosphere defend Earth from alien invaders? **Meteors** occur when bits of dust and rock, called meteoroids, fall to Earth from outer space at speeds of up to 160,000 miles per hour.

When a meteoroid hits the atmosphere, it becomes a meteor. Friction, or rubbing, between it and air molecules causes heat. The heat makes a flash of light streak across the night sky.

Sometimes small bits fall to Earth as meteorites. But most meteors burn up in the atmosphere. You'll see the most meteor activity during a meteor shower. Dates for three of the most active showers seen north of the equator are:

| SHOWER | DATES | PEAK |
| --- | --- | --- |
| Quadrantids | January 1–6 | January 4 |
| Perseids | July 25–August 18 | August 12 |
| Geminids | December 7–15 | December 14 |

Other showers occur too. Watch the news, or check with a local museum or astronomy group.

The best time and place to watch is after midnight in a dark, open area. Bring an adult along for safety. And bundle up warmly, especially during fall or winter.

mates might make you go green, and that's a good thing! Here are some things you should know. A regular toilet uses 8 gallons of water every time you flush. It's estimated that every day Americans use 4.8 billion gallons of clean water just to flush their toilets. That's almost half the water we use indoors every day!

And here's another great tip. If every home in the United States bought just one roll of 100 percent recycled paper towels, it would save more than a half million trees.

Did you know that every year we throw away 20 million tons of electronics, like old computers, radios, and CD players? Recycling really helps us save the planet! Recycling an aluminum can takes just 5 percent of the energy it takes to find that amount of new aluminum and shape it into a new can.

## Solar Power

Solar energy is a "renewable resource." This means that you can use it, and more is being made all the time. As long as the sun is shining, more energy will be there for us to use. Solar energy is collected for heating homes, businesses, and water. It's used to dry out agricultural grains like wheat and corn, herbs, and fruit. People use solar power to heat pools, greenhouses, and arboretums. Solar power charges emergency phones on American highways, keeps streetlights lit, and powers flashing road signs. Builders have even developed solar roof shingles!

Solar power can even be made into electricity. This is called *photovoltaics*. Photovoltaic energy is when sunlight is collected by a "solar cell" and then passed through a special "semiconductor" to create an electrical flow. This was actually discovered accidentally by researchers at the telephone company in 1954, who were looking at how silicon reacted to sunlight.

Many solar cells are connected together into larger groups of cells to collect more power. The more solar cells there are, the more "watts" of energy they collect. Solar cells are not mechanical, so they take no energy to run and no water or cooling to convert sunlight to electricity. They make no waste that has to be thrown away. This is a clean and renewable energy.

### Solar Power Problems

One problem with solar power is that it's not always sunny outside! Some places have more cloud cover that blocks sunlight, and of course there is no solar power collection at night. The ideal place for solar power is an area where there is little cloud cover, like a desert or other dry region that has some room for solar collectors to lie out and take in the sunshine. In the United States, the southwestern part of the country gets the most sun, so it's best for solar collection, but homes everywhere can benefit from some solar collection. Even just big, south-facing windows can bring solar heat into a home. This is called *passive solar* collection.

The other problem with solar power is that you need a big area facing the sun to collect it. On a single home, the collection area can be on a rooftop facing the sun, but what about a tall building with many apartments? Or a whole city? It takes space to collect solar power. It is hard for big power companies to collect and sell solar power because sunlight collection takes a lot of space. There were only 14 known large, solar electric generating units working in the United States in 2004, all of them in California and Arizona.

But since then, it's been slow going. Solar science has also only worked out how to make power out of about 25 percent of the sunlight we get. Solar science still has a long way to go to be the endless, clean, free power we hope it will be. But it's getting there!

**MEDIEVAL SOLAR ENERGY**

During the fifteenth century Leonardo da Vinci had already made plans for harnessing solar power in his notebooks.

## Water Power

Power from water can be made in many different ways. The most common way is through a hydroelectric dam. This is where a river is blocked until the water builds up into a large lake, or reservoir, behind a tall dam wall. The water is released through an opening over the dam and as it falls, it flows through a machine called a *turbine* and turns the propellers attached to an electric generator. This creates the electricity. The greater height from which the water falls, the more power it makes.

Natural waterfalls like Niagara Falls work in much the same way. The power in the falling water makes the generator work, which makes the electricity. It is gravity working on the water that gives us this power. Power lines connected to the generator carry the electricity where it needs to go.

Hyrdroelectric power is a clean and renewable power source. There is no pollution given off while using hydroelectric power. The reservoir behind the damn can be a place for people to swim, boat, and fish. Farmers can use some of the water for their fields. A dam, once built, can last for 100 years.

### The Dark Side of Dams

There are a few bad things about dams that are important to know. To build a hydroelectric dam, a large area must be flooded behind the dam to make the reservoir. Whole communities sometimes have to be moved to another place. Entire forests can be drowned. Rotting vegetation under the water can give off a gas called *methane*. The water released from the dam can be colder than usual, which can harm the plants, fish, and animals in the rivers downstream. It can also wash away riverbanks and scrape away life on the river bottoms. The worst effect of dams has been seen on salmon that have to travel upstream to spawn, or lay their eggs. If blocked by a

## FUN FACT

### A FISH WITH A LADDER

To protect salmon and other spawning fish that are blocked by dams, fish ladders were created. A fish ladder (also called a *fish way* or *fish pass*) is a man-made structure built around a dam to allow fish to still make their way upstream to spawn. These ladders are often a chain of low steps that the fish can leap up! The flow of water has to be just right to attract the fish to the ladder but not tire it out.

dam, the salmon life cycle (and that of many other fish) cannot be completed. To try to solve this, fish experts designed fish ladders to get fish over the dam.

## Harnessing the Wind

The wind is renewable energy because it never stops blowing! It flows around the planet pushed on by the uneven heating and cooling of the earth's surface. It is an endless supply of power, if only we can harness it.

As soon as men took to the ocean in boats they began using wind power for sailing. Then farmers fastened early wind turbines into windmills. They used them to grind grain and pull up water from wells. Even early lumber mills were powered by windmills. In the early 1900s, when electricity had not made it out to some of the ranches in the American west, ranchers put up small windmills to generate their own electricity.

Nowadays wind energy is mostly used for making electricity. The turning blades power a generator that turns the mechanical power into electricity. Modern windmills are called *wind machines,* and they are huge. One wind machine can be as tall as a 20-story building with 3 blades that are 200 feet long. They are placed in wide, open areas, often near the coast where the wind blows a lot of the time.

More and more states are starting to make wind farms to help supply people with the electricity they need. The state of California makes more than twice as much wind power as any other of the 30 states using it. But they only work when the wind is blowing!

### Ocean Breeze

Because of the wind stirred up off the ocean, many wind farms are being planned for offshore sites. According to wind

## FUN FACT

**WINDMILL HISTORY**

Holland is usually thought to be the pioneer of windmill technology, but during the sixth and tenth centuries people in Persia were using windmills to grind grain and pump water from wells. Windmills have also been used in China for over 2,000 years.

## DID YOU KNOW?

The fastest "normal" wind, meaning wind not related to a tornado or hurricane, was recorded at Mount Washington in New Hampshire in 1934. How fast was it? 231 miles per hour!

power experts, each windmill will be able to make up to 4 million kilowatt hours (kWh) of electricity per year. That will supply up to 400 homes.

Wind farms with dozens of wind machines can make electricity for entire communities. A wind farm in Texas has 46 wind machines that make enough electricity for 7,300 homes. Wind farms are usually owned by people or businesses, which then sell the power to public power companies. In the United States today, wind machines are making enough electricity to supply about 1.6 million homes. That may sound like a lot but in a country as big as ours, it is still less than 1 percent of the people. It is growing over time though. In just the last 10 years, the amount of wind power has grown 300 percent.

Long ago, people wondered about the size and shape of the Earth. They wanted to know what lands lay on other shores, who lived there, and what their lives were like. So they built ships to sail the seas and trekked across foreign lands to explore this big world. These explorers shaped the countries we know today. They marked borders, set up capitals, and created cities. But geography didn't end hundreds of years ago. There are geographers today who have the same curiosities. What does it take to be a geographer? It takes some special knowledge of Earth sciences such as biology and geology. It takes some knowledge of people sciences such as anthropology, which is the study of humans, past and present. Above all, it takes a deep desire to learn new things.

## The United States

Welcome to the United States of America, located between Canada and Mexico and between the Atlantic Ocean and the Pacific Ocean. The United States was originally settled by Native American peoples, and European settlers did not arrive until a few hundred years ago. That might sound like a long time, but it's nothing if you think like a geographer! People have come from all over the globe to work, study, and live here. The United States is the third-biggest country in the world in terms of land mass. Only Russia and Canada have more land. It also has the third-largest population in the world; only China and India have more people.

### Peaks and Valleys

Long ago, glaciers came through the Northeast and created mountain peaks and river valleys. The Appalachian range is a chain of mountains extending from Newfoundland in Canada

**DID YOU KNOW?**

Did you know that the largest wave ever surfed was 77 feet high? That's about as tall as an eight-story building! Surfer Mike Parsons caught the wave on January 5, 2008, at Cortes Bank, an underwater mountain range 100 miles off the coast of Southern California.

down to central Alabama in the southern United States, totaling 1,500 miles in distance. The range contains the highest peak in the northeast—Mount Washington in New Hampshire. At 6,148 feet, the mountain is famous for its highly unpredictable weather and wind gusts of more than 230 miles per hour!

### Water, Water Everywhere!

Now let's go to the border between New York and Ontario. Be sure to put on your rain jacket! A collection of waterfalls sits between the twin cities of Niagara Falls, Ontario, and Niagara Falls, New York. Can you guess what these waterfalls are called? If you guessed Niagara Falls, you're right! The Canadian Falls drop 170 feet, and the American Falls drop 70 to 110 feet. More than 6 million cubic feet of water fall over the top every minute during the day. The water is rushing very fast—more than 60 miles per hour at times.

### Farm Land and Badlands

Glaciers covered much of the Midwest during the last Ice Age, about 10,000 years ago. Their movement eroded the land beneath them and led to the flat, rolling landscape found in the Midwest. This resulted in excellent farmland with rich soil.

Climb up into the Black Hills of South Dakota and you'll see four presidents' faces staring down at you. You've found Mount Rushmore! Each face is 60 feet high. The sculptor, Gutzon Borglum, carved the faces into the hills from 1927 to 1941.

### Glades and Caves

In the southeast you'll find the great state of Florida. Florida's climate is tropical, which means there is a wet season. And boy, is the wet season wet! It rains most of the time

**FUN FACT**

**BIG FALL**

Niagara Falls is the second largest falls in the world. The largest is Victoria Falls in southern Africa. Even though Niagara Falls is large, it is really not that old. The Niagara River is only about 12,000 years old. That's only about a microsecond in geological time!

**FUN FACT**

**ARE BADLANDS BAD?**

The Badlands in North Dakota got their name because erosion in the southwest created jagged hills and deep valleys that were difficult to cross. This is how the area became known as the "bad" lands.

# Across the Ocean

**Before airplanes, there was only one way to get to faraway places.**
**Connect the dots to find out what it was!**

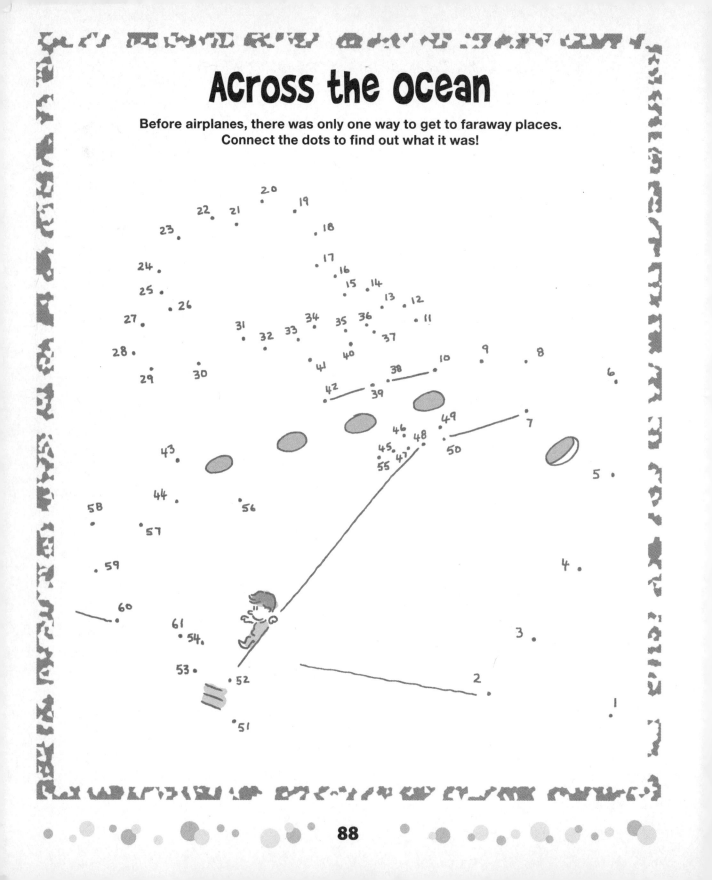

for 7 months, from April to October, and much of the rain comes from hurricanes and thunderstorms. In southern Florida, there is a wildlife refuge known as the Everglades that depends on this wet weather. Many kinds of mammals, birds, reptiles, and plants live in the Everglades.

Heading over to Kentucky, you can walk, crawl, and wiggle through big and small spaces in Mammoth Caves, the largest cave system in the world. These tunnels and rooms were formed over millions of years by water and limestone. Always go caving with a friend or two to be safe!

Kentucky also has a magical secret! In Cumberland Falls State Resort Park, on a clear night with a full moon, you can see a colorful moonbow arc over the falls and the gorge. You can't find a moonbow anywhere else in the Western Hemisphere!

### A Grand Landscape

The Colorado River has been rushing through the famous Grand Canyon for millions of years. The canyon is 227 miles long and about a mile deep. Temperatures and weather vary quite a bit here, making hiking tricky, but Grand Canyon National Park is one of the world's top tourist attractions with about 5 million visitors each year.

Over in New Mexico you can find the Carlsbad Caverns located in the Guadalupe Mountains. These caves were not formed by water and limestone like Mammoth Caves. Instead, they were formed from an acid called *sulfuric acid*. There are more than 100 caves in the Carlsbad Caverns National Park. Some of the caves have unusual names such as Balloon Ballroom, Chocolate High, Hall of the White Giant, and Spirit World.

## FUN FACT

### HIDDEN ISLAND?

All the Hawaiian islands were formed by eruptions from undersea volcanoes. Mount Kilauea is Hawaii's most active volcano. It has been erupting since 1983, and you can see it if you go to Volcanoes National Park. What you won't be able to see is a new Hawaiian island called *Loihi*. It's still forming underneath the surface of the Pacific, and it will take tens of thousands of years for the new island to reach the surface. So no one can move there just yet!

## FUN FACT

### WON'T YOU BE MY NEIGHBOR?

Alaska is located right next to Canada, and it's closer to Russia than to the rest of the United States. Actually, Alaska used to be part of Russia. The Russians sold it to the United States in 1867 for two cents an acre. That might not sound like a lot, but Alaska is so big that it cost the United States $7.2 million!

## FUN FACT

### NOISY ICE

Glaciers and icebergs can be very noisy. Drop several ice cubes into a glass of warm water. You may notice how they crack and make a popping noise when they do so. This is the same sound icebergs make as they fall off into the ocean—only icebergs are much, much louder!

### Crash! Boom! Splash!

Ever wonder why earthquakes happen more on the west coast than on the east coast? California, Oregon, and Washington lie over two different parts of the Earth's crust. When those parts move against each other, they cause earthquakes.

Volcanic eruptions have occurred here as well. The Cascade mountain range, which includes Mount St. Helens and Mount Rainier, are part of the Pacific Ring of Fire—a ring of volcanoes and mountains around the Pacific Ocean. The Cascade volcanoes are the cause of all recorded eruptions in the continental United States.

## Is Greenland Really Green?

Look on a map of North America. Notice that large island way up in the northeastern part of the continent? This is the island of Greenland, the largest island in the world.

Greenland is very cold. A typical day on Greenland may see temperatures around 14 degrees on the Fahrenheit scale. People who live there think it feels really warm on Greenland when it reaches into the fifties. Greenland is also very dry, so there is little snow.

Almost the entire island is covered in a giant sheet of ice. In some places, the ice can be nearly 2 miles thick! These giant ice sheets, or *glaciers*, sometimes slide along the continent until they reach the ocean. When the ice hits the ocean, icebergs form. The giant ice sheets and icebergs in Greenland make up nearly 10 percent of all the fresh water on Earth. That's a lot of frozen ice cubes!

If most of the island is covered in ice, how did Greenland get its name? If you hopped in your Viking ship and sailed for Greenland, the first part of the island you would see is the coast. The coastline is rocky, mountainous—and very green!

# Living Dangerously

Most earthquakes and volcanic eruptions occur in the Pacific Ring of Fire, but millions of people still live along this belt. People live in all kinds of funny places. Can you figure out where this boy and his cat live? Just connect the dots.

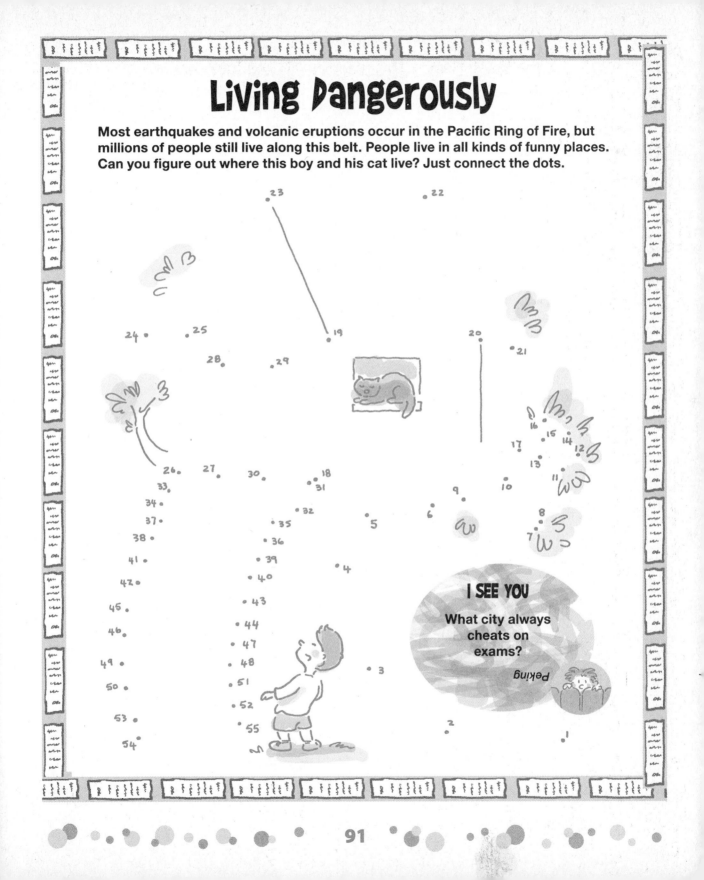

**I SEE YOU**

What city always cheats on exams?

Peking

## DID YOU KNOW? ........

Greenland is one of the best places in the world to see the Northern Lights (Aurora Borealis), one of nature's incredible forces. The Northern Lights form when charged protons and electrons emitted from solar winds are drawn in by Earth's magnetic field and crash into atoms and molecules in the atmosphere. These collisions create tons of bursts of red, green, pink, and purple lights!

This is why the island is called Greenland, even though the rest of the island does not exactly live up to its name. If you measured the length of the coastline of Greenland, you would find it is almost as long as the length of the equator!

During some winter months there are parts of Greenland that stay dark all day long, but during the summer, the opposite happens. There are days with no nights! Why do you think this is? You've probably noticed that it gets darker earlier during the winter than in the summer. The same thing happens in Greenland—it's just more extreme. In the winter, the Northern Hemisphere of the Earth is farther away from the sun, so it gets darker earlier. The farther north you are, the less light from the sun gets to you. In the summer, the Earth's orbit changes, and the northern hemisphere is angled toward the sun.

## The Andes

The Andes are found along the west coast of South America. They are more than 4,400 miles long, stretch as wide as 300 miles in places, and reach an average height of 13,000 feet above sea level. The Andes pass through 7 of the 12 South American countries: Argentina, Chile, Peru, Bolivia, Venezuela, Columbia, and Ecuador.

Remember when we talked about the Earth's tectonic plates? Well, the mountains were formed when two of the Earth's tectonic plates slammed into each other. In South America, two plates in the Pacific Ocean—the Nazca plate and the Antarctic plate—slipped under the South American plate, and this is how the Andes formed. But that's not all! Have you ever rubbed your hands together to keep them warm? Tectonic plates also create heat when one slips under the other. In the Andes, they created so much heat that part of the Earth's crust melted, allowing liquid magma to make its way to the surface. The result? Volcanic eruptions!

## DID YOU KNOW? ........

The volcanoes in the Andes are still active today. Cotopaxi is a volcano found in the Andes in the country of Ecuador. It is currently one of the most active volcanoes in the world.

The climate and plants and animals in the Andes vary depending on where you are, such as how close you are to the Pacific Ocean and how high above sea level you are. Animals such as alpaca, llama, and chinchillas are found in the Andes. Hummingbirds, quetzals, and toucans are birds that inhabit the trees and forests of the area. The Andes have dense deciduous forests, rainforests, and high mountain peaks with little vegetation (plants).

## European Landscape

Western Europe has extremes in temperatures, climates, peoples, and cultures. The reaches of Norway and Sweden are covered in frozen tundra (a treeless landscape filled with moss, some grasses, and small shrubs). Countries such as Portugal and Spain have beautiful warm beaches along the shores of the Mediterranean Sea. Many of the other countries of Western Europe are covered by the Alps, one of the major mountain ranges in Europe. France and Spain are separated by the Pyrenees Mountains.

The tiny country of Monaco, which takes up less than 1 square mile, is more crowded with people than any other country in the whole world. There are 32,543 people who call the country home, and they all live in an area that's roughly the size of Central Park in New York City! Compare that with Iceland, another Western European country. Iceland has only 7 people per square mile!

### FUN FACT

**MOUNTAINOUS AMOUNTS OF LIFE**

The Tropical Andes region has the greatest range of plants and animals in the world. So far, 45,000 species of plants have been described (15–17 percent of the world's plant species!) as well as 414 mammal species, 1,666 bird species, and 1,309 reptile and amphibian species. Can you imagine seeing all that life across one mountain range?

## FUN FACT

### EUROPEAN MUMMIES

Bog mummies or bog bodies are naturally preserved bodies of people who died thousands of years ago. These mummies are sometimes found in the sphagnum bogs of Northern Europe. The skin and internal organs on the bog mummies are perfectly preserved because of the unusual environment in the bog. In some cases these bodies still have all their hair and nails perfectly intact.

## DID YOU KNOW? ........

In October 2010, engineers working over 6,500 feet beneath the Swiss Alps blasted through the last remaining rock to create the Gotthard Rail Tunnel, the longest train tunnel in the world! It took 14 years to build this tunnel, and cost $10.3 billion. When the tunnel officially opens in 2016, it will take up to 300 trains a day!

### Fjord Alert!

Western Europe is dotted with fjords. A fjord is a steep, narrow valley carved out of rocks by glaciers. In most cases, a fjord is found near the inlet of a larger body of water. Most fjords reach deeper than sea level. Fjords are found in Ireland, Norway, Sweden, and Iceland. The Sognefjord in Norway is one of the world's largest fjords. It reaches more than 120 miles inland from the Atlantic Ocean and plunges to depths of close to 4,200 feet below sea level!

The rise and fall of the tides in a fjord are quite dramatic. Because of the high, steep walls and the fact that much of the fjord extends below sea level, the difference between high and low tides can be extreme. When the tide rises in the ocean connected to the fjord, the water rushes into the relatively small fjord. It is best to be prepared for this twice-daily event so you don't get stuck on the beach as the water rushes in!

### The Alps

The Alps are one of the major mountain ranges in of Europe. The Alps stretch from Austria to Italy and Switzerland and into France. The highest peak in the Alps is Mont Blanc. Mont Blanc (which means "white mountain") is between France and Italy. It reaches more than 15,800 feet into the sky. This makes it the eleventh tallest mountain the whole world.

The mountains of the Alps were carved by glaciers. These giant ice sheets carved out large basins in the mountains, changed river valleys, and smoothed the rocks there. You can still find mountain glaciers in some of the higher peaks in the Alps.

# Mini Mountain

The state of Louisiana has some of the lowest land in America. In fact, its highest mountain is only 535 feet above sea level. It is called Driskill Mountain, but it doesn't actually qualify as a mountain because it isn't tall enough. How high do you think it would have to be to qualify as a mountain? There are a lot of mountains in this puzzle, but only two of them are real. Can you see which ones have one cloud, snow, two peaks, and the sun setting on the west side?

## HIDING IN PLAIN VIEW

There are many towering mountains on earth that only a handful of people have ever seen, yet they are in plain view. How can that be?

*Some mountains rise thousands of feet, but they never rise above the ocean they are sitting in.*

## WHAT A PILE OF SAND!

The sand dunes in the Sahara are huge! Some of them are as tall as 600 feet. That is about half as tall as the Empire State Building in New York City.

## CAMELS

Dromedary camels, which live in Africa, have one hump, and Bactrian camels, which call Asia home, have two. The humps of a camel are used to store fat—not water like many people believe.

## Whew! It's Hot Here! A Look at the Sahara Desert

The Sahara Desert is in Africa and covers most of the countries of North Africa. This desert stretches from the Atlantic Ocean on the west to the Red Sea on the east. It reaches from the Mediterranean Sea in the north to Sudan in the south.

The Sahara is the second-largest desert in the world after the Gobi Desert in Asia. And the Sahara is getting bigger! Global warming and other climate changes are working together to expand the desert. It is believed that the desert expands southward at the rate of about 18.5 miles a year. This means that many people are losing their fields to the desert and many animals are losing their homes.

The Sahara Desert receives the greatest amount of possible sunlight of any place on Earth. The lack of clouds, storms, and pollution means that this area receives 4,300 hours of sunlight each year. So it's sunny 97 percent of the time!

The plants and animals of the Sahara are easily recognized. Mammals such as the dromedary camel and goats are herded and used for transportation, food, or milk. The hyrax, a small relative of the elephant, is found in the Sahara. Most of the plants in this desert are able to withstand droughts. Many of these plants have roots that stick deep down into the ground. In some cases, the roots may reach as far down as 80 feet! The roots travel so deep because they are trying to find water. Palm trees, cacti, and acacia trees are well suited for this desert environment.

## The Bottom of the World

The fifth-biggest continent in the world, Antarctica, is the coldest, driest, and windiest place on Earth. It is almost completely covered in the Antarctic ice sheet, which ranges from 1 to 3

# Longest Largest

Adventurous Dave has traveled all over Asia. He even kept records of how far he walked, but now he has to add them all up. Can you see which one of these 5 rivers is the longest?

Lena (Russia) 1000 + 500 + 500 + 500 + 236 = _____

Indus (Pakistan and India) 100 + 900 + 500 + 400 + 76 = _____

Yellow (China) 1000 + 1000 + 1000 + 397 + 1 = _____

Yangtze (China) 1000 + 500 + 2000 + 417 = _____

Volga (Russia) 500 + 500 + 500 + 500 + 266 = _____

## PEE-YEW!
*As well as being the longest river in Asia, the Yangtze River is often referred to as the dirtiest. It is believed that 90 percent of the water in the river is polluted.*

# FUN FACT

## BRRRRRRR!

The world's lowest recorded temperature was –129 degrees on the Fahrenheit scale, at Vostok Research Station in Antarctica in 1983. Inland temperatures can go down to –112 to –130 degrees in winter and coastal temperatures can go up to between 41 and 59 degrees in summer.

miles thick. There's a lot of frozen water in all that snow. But Antarctica is called a desert because it only gets a little precipitation (rain or snowfall)—about the same amount as the Sahara in Africa! One reason it's so cold in Antarctica, besides all the snow and ice, is that freezing winds called *katabatic winds* blow up to 200 miles per hour. These winds blow from high plateaus down onto the coasts and cause strong blizzards.

Antarctica has the world's largest ice shelves: the Ross Ice Shelf and the Filchner-Ronne Ice Shelf. An ice shelf is a thick section of ice that forms at the spot where a glacier or ice sheet meets the coastline. The Ross Ice Shelf is 2,300 feet thick in some places, and the Filchner-Ronne Ice Shelf is about 2,000 feet at its thickest. In summer, ice shelves melt and break away, forming icebergs. Some Antarctic icebergs are as big as 5,000 square miles.

# FUN FACT

## TROPICAL ANTARCTICA?

More than 500 million years ago, Antarctica was part of a larger land mass called *Gondwana,* and West Antarctica was north of the equator. The continent had a warm, tropical climate with all kinds of animals, including some dinosaurs!

CHAPTER 8

# Hysterical Happenings in American History

## DID YOU KNOW? ········

What's the biggest pumpkin you've ever seen? In Rhode Island in November 2007, a man named Scott Cully carved the largest jack o'lantern in the world—weighing in at 1,689 pounds! The Guinness World Records cites this as the largest jack o'lantern ever carved. You could make a lot of pies with that pumpkin!

# FUN FACT

## A LONG LAKE NAME

Lake Chargoggagoggman-chauggagoggchaubunagun-gamaugg is the longest name of any body of water in the United States. It is located in Webster, Massachusetts. It is a Native American name that means "You fish on your side and I'll fish on my side, and nobody fishes in the middle." It was probably named in honor of an agreement between two tribes.

The United States is a remarkable country, and many Americans feel lucky to live here. Have you ever wondered what this country is like? Maybe you know a bit about your neighborhood, your hometown, and even your home state, but there are 50 states in the United States. How much do you know about them?

Did you know that the state of Alaska would fill up one-fifth of the total area of the rest of the United States all by itself? Did you know that Massachusetts has a lake that has the longest name of any body of water in the whole United States? It's true! Let's find out what else is special about this country, from sea to shining sea!

## New England

Connecticut, Maine, Massachusetts, New Hampshire, Rhode Island, and Vermont make up the region we know as New England. New England includes some of the oldest states in the union. For example, Massachusetts was founded as a colony nearly 400 years ago. The American Revolution started in New England, as did the American anti-slavery movement nearly a century later.

Many of our country's leaders were born in New England, including revolutionary leaders like Samuel Adams, his cousin John Adams, and John's remarkable wife, Abigail. John Adams later became our second president. His son, John Quincy Adams, was also president. In the 1960s, Massachusetts senator and war hero John Fitzgerald Kennedy became the thirty-fifth president.

New England is famous for its seasons, especially for autumn, when the leaves in its huge forests turn different colors. People from all over the world come to New England in the fall to see the beautiful changing of the leaves. And did you know that they make maple syrup from the tree sap in the spring? Yum!

# Maple Magic

**Starting at number 1, connect the dots in order to find a maple surprise.**

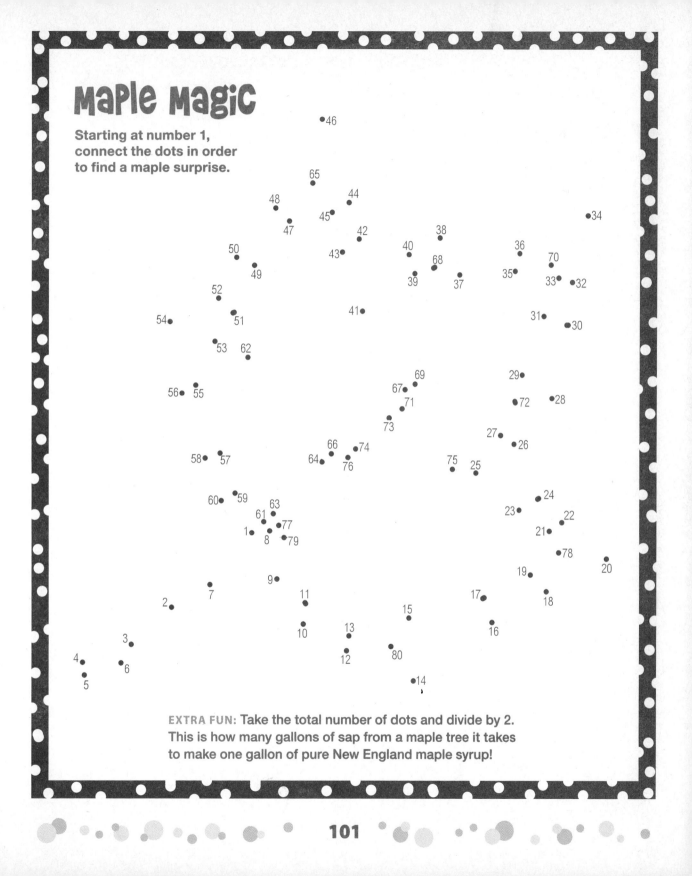

**EXTRA FUN:** Take the total number of dots and divide by 2. This is how many gallons of sap from a maple tree it takes to make one gallon of pure New England maple syrup!

# FUN FACT

## FLAVORFUL HISTORY

The legendary Ben and Jerry's ice cream began in 1978 in a rundown gas station in Burlington, Vermont. In 1983 Ben and Jerry's ice cream was used to build the world's largest ice cream sundae weighing 27,102 pounds!

## Fun New England Facts

The Battle of Bunker Hill was a famous battle fought not far from Boston, Massachusetts. In this battle, over a thousand British troops were killed by American militia units, which showed that the Americans could stand up to the British Army's best soldiers! But did you know that the Battle of Bunker Hill was not fought on Bunker Hill? It was actually fought on the next hill over, a place called Breed's Hill.

Did you know that Rhode Island's state bird is a chicken? It's true! Rhode Island is home to the famous breed of chicken known as the Rhode Island Red. This type of chicken is the state bird of Rhode Island.

Connecticut is home to Yale University, one of the most famous colleges in the world. Several presidents have attended Yale including President George H. W. Bush, President George W. Bush, President Bill Clinton for law school (after graduating from Georgetown University in Washington, D.C.), and President Gerald Ford for law school.

The Old Man of the Mountain was a New Hampshire rock formation that looked very much like the profile of an old man. New Hampshire residents adopted it as their state symbol in 1945. Unfortunately, the rocks that formed the natural sculpture had worn down over the years, and the entire structure collapsed in 2003.

Timber has always been a major export for Maine. During the Age of Sail (when people traveled mostly by sailing ships), Maine's tall white pine trees were used to make ships' masts, which hold up the sails. In fact, the very first sawmill in the United States was built in Maine, on the Piscataqua River in 1623.

## The Mid-Atlantic States

Many of the states in this region were among the original colonies that fought a war for independence from Great Britain and later ratified the U.S. Constitution.

The Mid-Atlantic States were also the birthplace of the westward settlement movement and the Transportation Revolution (1816–1850). These two sweeping events led to the beginnings of the railway, steel, coal, oil, and canal-building industries. As a result, some of the largest and most heavily populated cities in the United States are in the Mid-Atlantic States. Cities such as New York City, Philadelphia, Buffalo, Pittsburgh, and Baltimore all boomed in part because of their location during the Transportation Revolution.

### Fun Mid-Atlantic Facts

Remember when we talked about hydroelectric power and Niagara Falls? Well, the falls are a fun place to visit, too! In fact, the falls of the Niagara River in New York are a world-famous attraction that draws millions of people to see them every year. Every hour 5,000,000,000 gallons of water flow over the edge of the Niagara Falls. It is said that you can hear the falls from as far off as 10 miles away!

Millions of people who came to settle in America entered the country through Ellis Island, which is in New York Bay. These people were called *immigrants*, and the island was an immigration station for about 50 years, from the 1890s until it closed in 1943. A little less than half of Americans (40 percent) had an ancestor pass through Ellis Island!

Did you know that Philadelphia was the first capital of the United States? It's true! For a number of years both during and after the American Revolution, Philadelphia was our national capital. The capital moved to New York during President Washington's administration.

### DID YOU KNOW? • • • • • • • •

Did you know that President Thomas Jefferson kept grizzly bears as pets on the White House lawn? It's true! In 1807 explorer Captain Zebulon Pike sent Jefferson a gift of two grizzly bear cubs. The bears grew quickly and soon were too big for their cages, so Jefferson kept them in a pen on the White House lawn. Jefferson eventually sent the bears to his friend Charles Willson Peale for his Philadelphia museum.

### FUN FACT

**IROQUOIS LANGUAGE**

The Iroquois language has no sounds that are made with your lips pressed together! Their names for themselves, as well as the rest of their language, do not include sounds like "m," "b," or "p." That is why they have names like Ho-de-no-sau-nee, and Hiawatha.

Most states have a state song, a state bird, a state tree, and a state flower. Hawaii even has a state fish. But can you name the state drink of even one of the United States? Well, now you can! Delaware has a state drink—it's cow's milk, of course! What could be more American than that?

Did you know that Delaware was the first of the original 13 colonies (later the first 13 states) that won their independence from England to ratify the U.S. Constitution? It's true! The people of Delaware are to this day very proud to call theirs the "first state," because of this!

## The Upper South

Have you ever had Kentucky Fried Chicken? Well, can you guess where it originally came from? The Upper South is where much of what is called "southern cooking" comes from. Recipes for meals like mac 'n' cheese, chicken and dumplings, and fried chicken were created in this region. Yum!

Some of the states in the Upper South have been called the *Border States,* because they run along the Mason-Dixon Line, which runs along Pennsylvania's border with Maryland, then along the Ohio River, all the way to the Mississippi. This line was originally established to end an argument over state boundaries between Maryland and Pennsylvania. But it is also well known for dividing the free states from the slave states until the Civil War.

All of these Border States participated in the Civil War, and almost all of them had their citizens fighting on both sides in that terrible struggle. The main reasons the Civil War was fought between the North and the South were questions like whether individual states had the right to make laws that were not allowed by the national government, and whether the practice of slavery ought to be kept (as many Southerners thought) or whether it ought to be stopped (as many Northerners thought). In the end, the Northerners won, and the South remained part of the United States.

### Fun Upper South Facts

Kitty Hawk is the site of the first airplane flight in 1903. Two Ohio bicycle shop owners named Orville and Wilbur Wright used the strong winds of Kitty Hawk to help them get their first airplane off the ground. Today you can see the Wright Brothers' airplane at the Smithsonian Institution in Washington, D.C.

The Appalachian Trail passes through 14 states and runs between northern Georgia and Maine. Every year, millions of hikers and campers visit parts of the trail. Some people actually hike the whole thing from one end to the other. This is a real accomplishment, because the Appalachian Trail is over 2,000 miles long!

Did you know that at one time the French owned more of North America than either the Spanish or the English? Then the French lost a war with England, and it cost them all of their land in North America, including Canada, all of the land around the Great Lakes, and all of the land that had rivers that ran into the Mississippi. Of course, Kentucky was part of this territory.

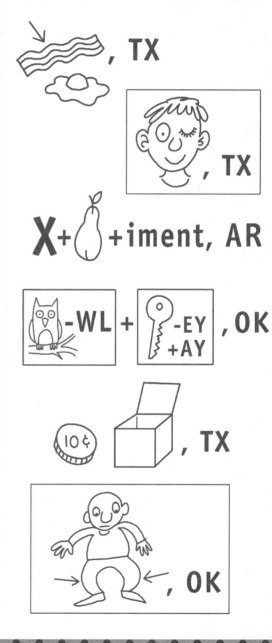

# You Live Where?

Figure out the word equations and picture puzzles to learn some silly but real names for cities in the Southern Plains!

# One to Grow On

Two sisters from Louisville, Kentucky, wrote a simple song in 1893.
Every single person you know can sing this song and knows all the words!
What is it? To find out, fill in all the boxes with a dot in the center.

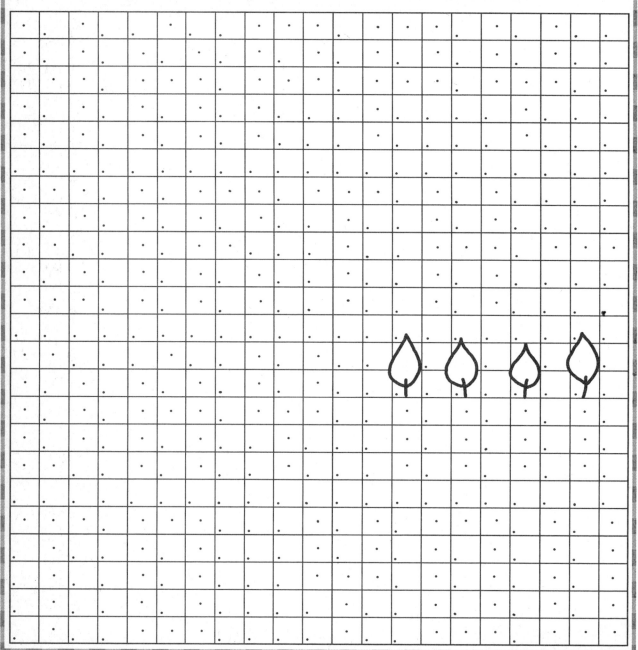

## The Deep South

Swamps. Mint juleps. Moss-covered plantation houses. These are the images that come to mind when people think of the Deep South. And yet there is so much more to the Deep South than that! Florida has long beaches, a colorful Caribbean sub-culture, and Disney World in Orlando. South Carolina has gorgeous beaches as well, with Myrtle Beach being one of its most famous.

And the food! If you like it deep-fried, you'll like the Deep South! They even deep-fry vegetables in the Deep South (like fried okra). And then there's the barbecue, and the cornbread! Get out the napkins, please!

The Deep South is a large area and is filled with many contrasts. It has mountains and lowlands, swamps and prairies, forests and bayous. It is also a land of large, powerful rivers such as the Mississippi, Alabama, Tennessee, and Tombigbee.

### Fun Deep South Facts

During the first years of the revolution, South Carolina did not see much action aside from hit-and-run raids by rebel units on British forces. The leaders of these rebel units became famous for their ingenuity and daring. Men such as Francis Marion (so crafty that he was nicknamed the Swamp Fox) and Thomas Sumter, with their cunning, Native American-style tactics, helped change the way wars were fought.

Have you ever heard about St. Augustine in Florida? It is the oldest city in North America. Spanish settlers established it in 1565!

Did you know that Richmond, Virginia, was not the original capital of the Confederate States of America? It's true! Because Virginia did not secede from the Union until many months after the states of the Deep South did, the capital was originally located in Montgomery, Alabama.

### DID YOU KNOW?

The biggest cookie ever created was made in the United States—it weighed 40,000 pounds and was 101 feet long! The Immaculate Baking Company in Flat Rock, North Carolina, baked this beauty on May 17, 2003. You'd need a lot of milk for that cookie!

### FUN FACT

**THAT'S NUTTY!**

Do you like peanuts? If you do, odds are that the ones you've eaten came from Georgia. Georgia is the country's largest producer of peanuts. Former president (and Georgia resident) Jimmy Carter started out as a peanut farmer.

# Pickles?

Of all the states, Georgia is the biggest producer of the "three Ps." Follow the directions on the right to cross items out of the grid. When you are done, you will know what the three Ps are!

| | | |
|---|---|---|
| POMEGRANATES | PEAS | PAPAYAS |
| PARSNIPS | PEANUTS | PEARS |
| PECANS | PENCILS | PEPPERS |
| PALMETTOS | PIMENTOS | PUMPKINS |
| PASTA | PUZZLES | PRETZELS |
| POPCORN | PORK | PINEAPPLES |
| PAPRIKA | PENNIES | PLOWS |
| PATIOS | POTATOES | PEACHES |
| PICKLES | PUDDING | PASTRIES |
| PLUMS | PETUNIAS | PANCAKES |

Cross out all items that...

...are not edible

...have double letters

...start with PA

...have the letter K

...are less than 6 letters

...are more than 7 letters

...have the letter O

## The Midwest

The Midwestern states might also be called the Great Lakes states, because each of them (even the mostly land-locked Indiana) at least partially borders the Great Lakes. Such large continental rivers as the Ohio and the Mississippi are also important in tying the states of this region together.

Most of the states of the Midwest are part of what is now known as the Rust Belt, as well. This is a part of the country that built up huge manufacturing plants because of its closeness to coal and oil deposits, its central location, and its good transportation routes to other parts of the country (first by riverboat, then by railroad) and to the world.

Several of the cities in this section of the country have been very important to the development of American industry, including Detroit, Cleveland, Milwaukee, and especially Chicago. The Midwest region of the country ties the other sections together.

### Fun Midwest Facts

Ohio has supplied more presidents to our country than any other state, eight presidents in all! Aside from William Henry Harrison (who was born in Virginia, and moved to Ohio when it was still a territory), all of these presidents were born and raised in Ohio: Ulysses S. Grant, Rutherford B. Hayes, James A. Garfield, Benjamin Harrison, William McKinley, William Howard Taft, and Warren G. Harding.

Perhaps Wisconsin's most famous industrial product is the Harley-Davidson motorcycle. The Harley-Davidson company was founded in Racine, Wisconsin, in 1903. That year it produced three motorcycles. Since then, it has produced hundreds of thousands of motorcycles!

Minnesota's nickname, the "Land of 10,000 Lakes" is a mis-name. There are actually more than 10,000 lakes in Minnesota. In fact, there are over 12,000 in the state. This means that whoever came up with Minnesota's nickname got it wrong by over 2,000 lakes!

## FUN FACT

### POP HISTORY

Native Americans had popcorn as part of their daily diet nearly 80,000 years ago! In fact, there was a bag of popcorn brought to the first Thanksgiving. This led to the first American cold cereal: popcorn with milk poured over it, served at breakfast.

## The Northern Plains

Stretching unbroken from the Canadian border in the north down to the Oklahoma country in the south, the Great Plains both divide and bind together the North American continent. This part of the country is now known as America's Breadbasket because it grows enough grain collectively to feed the people of the world several times over. Wheat, oats, barley, and corn are grown all over the Great Plains.

And yet most people once called this region the Great American Desert! Before the steel plow was invented, there wasn't any blade strong enough to cut through the prairie sod of the plains, and so Americans viewed the Great Plains as an obstacle to be crossed on their way to places on the West Coast, like California.

The plains states are places of wide skies and broad horizons, of sudden tornadoes and baking hot, cloudless days. They are bordered by huge mountains in the west, and the broad Mississippi in the east. And they are crossed from northwest to southeast by a number of vast river systems of their own.

### Fun Northern Plains Facts

In the 1880s future U.S. President Theodore Roosevelt established a working cattle ranch in the badlands of western North Dakota. Roosevelt spent three years working as a cowboy on his own ranch. He identified himself as a cowboy at heart for the rest of his life!

Did you know that there is a railroad that has a 60-degree grade (that is *steep!*) and is less than 300 feet long? It's true! The world's shortest railroad is in Dubuque, Iowa, and measures only 296 feet!

Lincoln, Nebraska, isn't just an important city in the insurance industry and home to the University of Nebraska Cornhuskers football team. It is also home to the world's only roller-skating museum!

## The Southern Plains

The Southern Plains stretch from Missouri into Colorado, from the Gulf of Mexico to the Guadalupe Mountains in the west. They are broad and flat in places, rolling and hilly in others, and they rise into interesting rock formations and tablelands called *mesas* in others.

The Southern Plains experience serious extremes of temperature over the course of the year: cold in the winter and blazing hot in the summer. They are subject to some of the worst hailstorms and tornadoes in recorded history. These states have amazing mineral wealth, including oil, natural gas, and coal. They have rich farmland, and a couple of them (Louisiana and Texas) have huge and interesting populations.

The Southern Plains are also a rich mix of different cultures. Originally settled in places by the French and Spanish (and the Mexicans), and occupied continuously in others by a variety of Native American cultures, these states are a fascinating mosaic of the diversity the United States is capable of, even while the skyline seems unrelentingly the same throughout the region.

### Fun Southern Plains Facts

When Missouri was ready to become a state, it turned out that it was a few thousand people short of the number required to become a state. So Congress shaved off what we now call the "bootheel" from the Arkansas Territory, and added it to Missouri in order to make its population high enough to qualify it for statehood!

Crayfish are freshwater lobsters. They are smaller than their ocean-going cousins, and are highly prized by Cajun cooks. Nearly 100 percent of all crayfish caught and eaten in the United States are caught in Louisiana!

**DID YOU KNOW?**

The Mississippi River is the largest river in North America; it begins in Minnesota and flows south to Louisiana, emptying out in the Gulf of Mexico. It's the fourth longest river in the world, at about 2,320 miles long!

Cajuns have a distinctive dialect of French, and also a distinctive culture, including their world-famous Cajun cooking. This food is heavy on the use of such Louisiana staples as rice and seafood, and is heavily spiced. Some Cajun food is so hot it could make your tongue dial the fire department, so be careful when you try it!

## The Intermountain West

Imagine a region with a skyline of jagged peaks that reach higher skyward than anywhere else in the continental United States. This is a place of broad plains and wide, rapid-running rivers, where everything is giant-sized. This is the Intermountain West, and the mountains are the Rockies.

Nothing is small in the Intermountain West. These mountains make mountains elsewhere in the country (like the eastern seaboard) seem more like hills. All of the large rivers that flow eastward across the Great Plains and into the Mississippi originate in the Intermountain West. Rivers such as the Missouri, the Arkansas, the Red, the Canadian, the Platte, and the Rio Grande all begin in the Rocky Mountains. So do the two great rivers of the west—the Colorado in the southwest and the Columbia (which rises in the Canadian Rockies) in the northwest.

### Fun Intermountain West Facts

Do you know about Old Faithful, the world-famous Yellowstone geyser? It was named Old Faithful because it was thought to be so reliable. Well, it's not! Old Faithful erupts in a tall cascade of water *on average* every 65 minutes, but it doesn't erupt nearly that regularly. The time between its eruptions can run anywhere from 30 to 90 minutes.

Can you guess what the deepest canyon in North America is? It's not the Grand Canyon or Bryce Canyon—it's Hells Can-

### FUN FACT

### HOME OF THE SPUD

Do you like French fries? Then more than likely you have eaten an Idaho potato, because Idaho leads the country in potato production. Many scientists think that potatoes do so well in southern Idaho because the climate is very similar to the climate in the Andes, which is where the first potatoes grew.

yon in Idaho. At one point this canyon runs nearly 8,000 feet below the mountain peaks that surround it. You could stack five and a half Empire State Buildings in a canyon that deep!

America has apartment houses all over it, in every city and in most towns, even the smallest ones. But what were the first apartment houses on this continent? They were built against steep canyon walls in the American Southwest by an ancient people called the Anasazi. These buildings were constructed of a type of mud brick called *adobe,* and they were several stories high!

### CLIMB ON UP

The Anasazi people used ladders to get into their cliff homes. Anytime they were under an enemy attack they would simply raise the ladders, keeping their homes and families safe.

## The Southwest

Sweeping from the borders of the southern plains all the way to the Pacific Ocean, the states of the Southwest are made up of vast deserts, high mountains, large rivers, and magnificent forests. This is the region that houses the mighty Grand Canyon and the ancient Sequoia trees of northern California, the wide Mojave Desert, and both the high Rocky Mountains and the rugged Sierra Nevada.

The Southwest has states with small populations, such as New Mexico, and the state with the largest population, California. It is both incredibly rural, with thousands of square miles where no human lives, and also incredibly urban. Orange County in California, for example, has more people living there than live on the entire continent of Australia!

There are rivers such as the Rio Grande, the Colorado, and the Sacramento running through the Southwest, and rain into the Gulf of Mexico, the Gulf of California, and the Pacific Ocean. The Pacific Ocean runs

along the western edge of the region, and on that coast there are fine natural harbors such as San Francisco Bay, Drake's Bay, and San Diego Harbor, to name just a few.

## Fun Southwest Facts

The Carlsbad Cavern system in New Mexico contains over 80 different caves, including Lechuguilla Cave, which is the deepest cave in the United States! It was discovered in 1986, and has been measured down to a depth of nearly 1,567 feet (That is deeper than a 110-story skyscraper!). It has not been completely explored yet, so it might be even deeper!

Did you know that wood can become stone? Sometimes dead wood (such as a fallen log) is covered over with mud that contains volcanic ash. Over time, elements in the ash and mud replace the wood's cells, but keep its shape, so the rock develops in the form of the wood. When that happens to wood, it's called *petrification*. The Petrified Forest in Arizona has one of the largest collections of petrified trees in the world!

People such as the Earp brothers, led by the famous Wyatt Earp, came to Arizona looking to get rich quick. The Earps eventually got into a power struggle with another local family, the Clantons. This power struggle led to the most famous gunfight in western history: the gunfight at the OK Corral!

Did you know that both the highest and the lowest points in the continental United States are in California? Mount Whitney, which measures 14,494 feet, is less than 90 miles from Death Valley, which is the lowest point at 282 feet below sea level. Death Valley has also had the highest recorded temperature in the United States at 134 degrees Fahrenheit in 1913!

**DID YOU KNOW?**

Each evening in the summer you can watch the almost 400,000 bats exit the Carlsbad Caverns in search of some tasty insects.

# CHAPTER 9
# Baffling Bugs and Creepy Crawlies

**A**re you into creepy, crawly, slimy, squirmy, squishy, squashy fun? Bugs, as you know, are everywhere—in the air, in the water, in the earth, and all around you. Hundreds of thousands of these creatures have been discovered over the years and even more are found each year!

## Wasps and Spitballs

What do wasps have to do with spitballs? Well, if you've ever made a spitball, you know that by chewing up a piece of paper you change it into a whole new object. Of course, the only reason kids make spitballs is to shoot them at someone or something, which usually gets them in trouble. Well, wasps make spitballs too, but they have a much better reason for doing that. They actually use their spitballs to make wasp nests.

# HiDing in a HoneycomB

There are six bugs hiding in this honeycomb. Can you find them? Start at any letter and move one space at a time in any direction. Once you've found all the bugs, see what other words you can make.

A wasp's paper nest is actually made out of small bits of chewed-up wood and saliva—a fancy name for spit! Other wasps prefer to build their homes out of mud or in the ground. No matter where you find them, wasps will protect their homes, and the way they defend them is by stinging, so don't get too close!

Wasps and bees may have been the first inventors of fans and air conditioning. As temperatures soar outside, you will find the bees and wasps fanning their homes with their wings. The fast movement of their wings cools the nest, making it more comfortable for the queen and the eggs that have not hatched yet.

## The Walking Stick

No, a walking stick really isn't a stick that can walk. And it's not a cane to help you walk, either. It's a bug! Walking sticks do look like sticks, and for a very good reason—that's how they hide. In fact, their disguise works so well, these creatures have been around for more than 4 million years.

Not all bugs have remained the same for so long. As time passes, many bugs have mutated (changed form) in order to adapt to their new surroundings. People adapt over time too! Take your messy room for example. You have probably adapted to it. (Your parents, on the other hand, probably never will.)

A walking stick spends most of its day in a balancing act of survival. Imagine avoiding hungry birds, pretending you're a stick anytime someone comes around, and hanging on for dear life when a storm comes. It sort of makes you appreciate how much easier it is to be a person.

### FUN FACT

**DIZZYING ACROBATICS**

If you watch a moth flying toward a light, you will notice that it spirals or circles until it reaches the light. The moth will turn in the direction of the light that is shining the brightest toward its closest eye. Depending on which direction the moth comes upon the light, it may spiral left or right.

### Walk Like a Walking Stick

If you're still curious what it feels like to be a walking stick, try walking a balance beam. For beginners, the best beam is a regular 2 × 4 board. Lay the board flat on its 4-inch side (for those of you who are carpenters, it's actually only 3½ inches long). With some practice you should be able to advance to the 2-inch side (which is really only 1½ inches). This requires bracing the beam with 8-inch pieces of board screwed on to each end to keep the beam from tipping over (ask your parents to help you out with this). Once you've mastered the balance beam, it's time to add a few more things, creating an obstacle course. If you are inside, you can use items like pillows, cushions, tables, footstools, blankets, or anything else you want to crawl through, in, on, or over. Moving outdoors allows for small slides, big boxes, planks, tires, and more. There's no limit to the obstacles you can add, so be creative, but keep everyone's safety in mind!

## Mole Crickets and Cave Mazes

Are you afraid of the dark? Most people are, even if they won't admit it. Imagine if you loved the dark. Some insects do, and a mole cricket is one of them. Because they like the dark, mole crickets are seldom seen, unless you happen to be digging in the ground where they live. Mole crickets use their shovel-like legs to dig their nests and to find buried food. They eat earthworms and other insects found underground. A mother mole cricket is very protective of her young. Once her eggs are laid she stays with them until they hatch.

### Magnetic Maze

If you are looking for a game that can test your friends' skills, try a magnetic maze. Find a smooth paper plate and draw

# What's the Difference?

To solve this puzzle, figure out where to put the scrambled letters. They all fit in spaces under their own column. When you have correctly filled in the grid, you will have the answer to the riddle.

HINT: The letters only form words horizontally. Use each letter only once.

## What's the difference between a coyote and a flea?

| ☒ | T | E |   | ☒ |   | ☒ | Y |   |   |   |   |   |   |
|---|---|---|---|---|---|---|---|---|---|---|---|---|---|
| T | N | E |   | R | A | P | R | ☒ |   | ☒ |   | O | ☒ |
| O | R | ☒ | I | H | I | E | R | A | W | O | S |   | T | E |
| P | H | H | E | H | O | ☒ | L | S | N | L | N | T | H | N | E |
| O |   |   |   |   | W |   |   |   |   |   |   | H |   |
|   | A |   |   |   |   |   | D |   |   |   |   |   |   |
|   |   |   | R |   | O |   |   |   |   |   |   |   |   |
|   |   |   | I |   |   |   |   |   |   |   |   |   |   |

your maze on top (a permanent marker will work best). Then, follow the marker lines this time with a bead of white glue. For heavy lines you may want to apply several coats of glue, one at a time as they dry. The bug you race can be made from a metal washer—decorate it with a bug sticker or a cutout. Using a fairly strong magnet on the underside of the plate, you can "race" the bug through the maze, to see who can get to the end fastest.

## Termites and Destruction

You're walking across a floor that you've walked across hundreds of times before, when suddenly a board falls in and you discover you have termites. These demolition experts prey on unsuspecting homeowners who seldom ever see them until it's too late. So, why do they want to eat you out of your home? It's simple, really—they're hungry.

Picture yourself with the appetite of a termite. It's after school, you're starving, and you see a piping hot chocolate chip cookie just lying there. What would you do? Termites eat wood

## FUN FACT

### VORACIOUS APPETITES

Some insects will eat almost anything, even dead animals. In fact, these creatures are the cleanup crew of the animal world—and you'd be amazed how quickly they can turn a dead rodent into a pile of bones.

and make tunnels within wooden boards to build their homes. Because they spend much of their time underground, most termites are light in color and have no wings. Termites are actually quite small, about the size of a grain of rice. Soldier termites protect the nest by shooting a nasty fluid out of their snout at anyone who tries to enter it. And worker termites care for the needs of the queen, the king, and the baby termites.

### Try Some Termite Destruction!

You can learn a lot about construction and destruction from a termite. From studying termites, people have learned what makes a structure weak and what makes it strong. To test this knowledge firsthand, you will need two large blocks of Styrofoam. Try standing on one. If it's big enough, it should be able to support you. Now take the other block and with the help of a parent, poke several holes all over it with a long nail or a drill (this will make a mess, so taking your experiment outside is a very good idea). Now try to stand on this block again. What happens? The block crumbles under pressure. And that's what happens when termites tunnel back and forth through the wood. If they are not stopped, they'll eat it all up, leaving nothing but a pile of wood dust.

In sandy places, termites are forced to build their homes out of dirt and sand. Some of these homes reach as high as 30 feet. These termite towers throw large shadows that could be used as sundials. Termites will also tunnel great distances underground to find wood. If a termite sees sunlight, it will die within a few hours. Termites require moisture and darkness in order to survive.

# FeeD Me

I am a plant that eats flesh. I like ants, spiders, and juicy bugs. When an insect lands in my open mouth—SNAP! I slam shut and trap the bug inside where it is slowly digested. Use a dark color to fill in the shapes that have the letters F-E-E-D M-E. The leftover white shapes will show what kind of predatory plant I am.

## Farming Pests

Now, it's time to leave the comforts of your home and travel to the countryside. Have you ever visited a farm? Let's say you are a farmer. You till the land, plant your seeds, and then hope for sunshine and rain. Nothing to it, really, right? Well, not exactly. Once you've finished planting, you need to take care of the small plants that sprout from the ground—they need your protection from weeds and, of course, from hungry bugs! And you'd be surprised what a menace these bugs can be. Bugs like the grasshopper will eat everything in their path. Sure, a few bugs can't eat very much. But once they invite all their bug friends to share the crops, watch out—hundreds of bugs can consume an entire field of corn or beans and many other types of crops.

Because insects may destroy crops, one natural way of dealing with them is crop rotation. Here is how it works: You switch what you grow on a particular field from year to year. Let's say you grow soybeans, and bugs that just love soybeans come and live in your field. Next year, if you plant soybeans again, there'll be even more of those bugs, and your crop will most likely be destroyed. If, however, you switch to growing broccoli next year, those bugs will decide that this kind of food is not for them, and will move on in search of food elsewhere. And by the time those bugs that love broccoli figure out that you've got it right there in your field, it'll be almost time for the harvest.

Here's how bugs can destroy a whole field of corn. When the corn plants first start to grow, they are invaded by billbugs, which drill holes in the corn stalks. Then, the European corn borers take over. Starting with the whorl, corn borers move down into the center of the plant, eating through the base of the stalks and finally getting to the corn ears. And when they finish their meals, leaving nothing but destroyed corn plants behind them, the corn borers emerge as full-grown moths, ready to lay eggs for the next year's generation.

**FUN FACT**

**BUG OLYMPICS**

Every year, Purdue University hosts the Bug Bowl, complete with cockroach-racing competitions. If you think you'll be in Indiana during April, why not stop by to cheer for your favorite bugs?

## Amazing Butterfly Facts

Butterflies can taste with their feet and they can hear and smell with their antennae. A butterfly cannot harm anything because it is unable to bite or chew. It only has a tongue called a *proboscis* that curls and uncurls like a party blower to sip nectar. Butterflies are characterized by their scale-covered wings. A butterfly's feathery scales come in all shapes and colors. The combination of veins and scales make the butterfly able to fly and glide. In fact, over time, people have learned a lot from these creatures.

Can you guess which insect may have inspired the following inventions?

- Gliders
- Needles
- Tunnels
- Nets
- Helicopters
- Camouflage
- Hammocks
- Straws
- Flashlights
- Apartment houses
- Tents

There is another reason why butterfly wings are special. Whether you are looking at the smallest butterfly (a dwarf blue), which is ½ inch in size, or the gigantic white birdwing butterfly (over 12 inches tall), every one is different. The patterns on the butterfly wings are as individual and unique as snowflakes—there are no two that are exactly alike.

### Make Your Own Magnification

To examine the little butterfly wings, you will need a microscope or a magnifying glass. If you don't have either one of these, how about making your own magnifying tool? It's actually very easy. What you need is a clear plastic egg or trinket holder (the kind that comes out of a toy machine) or a clear plastic soft drink bottle. If you pour a little water into the bottom of one of these and then hold it over a bug or some of the words in this book, you will see them better.

## FUN FACT

**GOING TO THE MOON**

Most of the time moths fly in a straight line, guided by the light of the moon. However, when they see our lights, they get confused by these impostor moons and try to switch course, which causes them to fly in circles. You can try to confuse moths even further by flashing two flashlights on and off, one at a time. If you succeed in tricking the poor moth, you'll see it flying back and forth from one flashlight to the other.

ET
ED
SU
NU
JU
ER
RO
LE
BA
Y
ED
EST
DRA
HU
AGE

_____ GG _____
_____ GG _____
GG _____
_____ GG _____
GG _____
_____ GG _____
GG _____
_____ GG _____
_____ GG _____
GG _____
_____ GG _____

FO
LL
LE
BI
E
LER
GI
WI

# Got Maggots?

The larvae of a Blow-fly can be placed in a deep wound where they eat dead tissue and kill harmful bacteria. The maggots in this wound have eaten away all the letters except for the GGs. Use the letters and letter pairs scattered around the page to fix the words.

**HINT:** Some letters make sense in more than one word, but there is only one way that uses all the letters.

## The Ant World

Did you know that there are 2,500 different kinds of ants? Some of the more famous ones are the fire ant, the army ant, and the honeypot ant. The fire ant gets its name from its terrible burning sting that is as painful to a human as a sting of a wasp or a bee. The army ant marches like the soldiers of a real army. They also fight and hunt for prey. The honeypot ant serves the purpose of storage in its colony—its abdomen is the pot that stores honey. When the honeypot ant's abdomen is filled with honey, it can reach the size of a cherry. Unable to move from the great weight, the ant just hangs there, from the roof of the nest, feeding the other ants in times of need.

### The Power of Communication

Ants have a very advanced communication system—they can talk to each other and give directions to where the food is, and they are also able to learn from their experiences. To see this higher-level thinking in action, all you have to do is have a picnic. Before long, these bugs will be joining you for a free lunch. And if you're not careful, they'll haul most of it off while you're not looking. Time to run and hide? Just try moving the picnic over a few feet. Still, before long they'll figure it out. Many people believe insects can't really think—they are just following their natural instincts. All living creatures have natural instincts, including you. A few common instincts are:

◆ Respecting or fearing water
◆ Looking for food
◆ Finding shelter in a storm
◆ Knowing when you're about to get in trouble

## Find Food Like an Ant

Ants look for food with the help of their antennae, which they use to smell. Sounds easy? Why not try it for yourself? Here is how you can have an ant treasure hunt. Wear a blindfold as you hunt for a strong-smelling food like fresh-baked cookies or fresh strawberries. (Of course, you will need a person who is not blindfolded to hide the food and then help you move around as you search for it.)

## Superb Digging Techniques

Many bugs use their mouths to dig; they also use their snouts, legs, feelers, and tails. Maybe you've heard the expression, "Okay, everybody, dig in" used at mealtime before? Well, most bugs do just that. They dig in, drill in, or bore their way through to a meal.

A mother acorn weevil makes a reservation for her babies' dinner in advance. First, she drills a hole into the acorn, and then she drops her babies down inside. If you find an acorn in the fall with a small hole in it, there may be weevils for you to see in the spring. Leave the acorn outside throughout the winter. Then gently open it in the early spring. The weevil you are looking for will have a really long snout.

## FUN FACT

### DRASTIC MEASURES

Did you know that several people have survived in the wild by eating insects until they were rescued? Although insects may not be as delicious as chocolate cake and ice cream, they do have nutritional value and can keep a person alive for a long time.

## Eggs for Safekeeping

Many insects lay eggs, which then hatch into fully grown bugs or into grubs. Often, these eggs need time to hatch, and many insects hide them by burying them in the ground. Other insect parents lay the eggs on carcasses of dead animals; still others are laid in an animal that's still living. The dung beetle (also known as a scarab beetle) has its own interesting approach to laying eggs. For thousands of years, these beetles have been rolling up balls of dung (droppings of other animals) and laying their eggs inside them. When the grubs hatch, they dine on the dung! Ewwwwww!

And yet, despite this behavior, the scarab beetle was considered to be sacred by the ancient Egyptians. According to them, the scarab beetle had the responsibility of rolling around the ball that represented the sun, and so it was worshipped as a god that made the sun rise in the mornings and set at night. You can still see many images of the scarab beetle in the ancient drawings and jewelry of the Egyptians.

**DID YOU KNOW?**

In your lifetime, you'll eat about 14 bugs in your sleep! The warmth and moistness of your mouth attracts them, and they usually never make it out.

## Sneaky Spiders and Other Traps

Ever heard of trapdoor spiders? These creatures take disguise to a whole new level—they construct a silk-hinged door that tricks their victims inside their house. The trapdoor opens

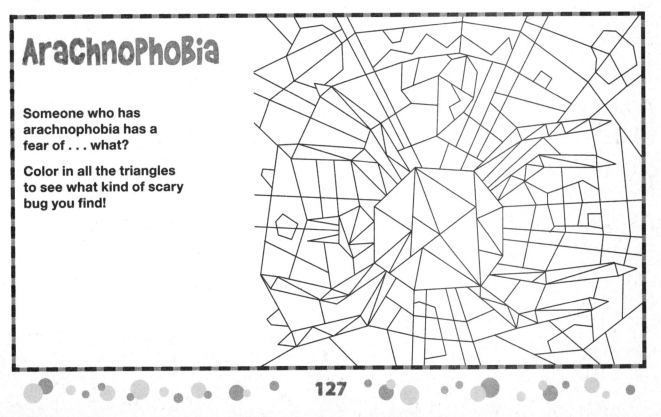

## Arachnophobia

Someone who has arachnophobia has a fear of . . . what?

Color in all the triangles to see what kind of scary bug you find!

## MICROSCOPIC MITES

The smallest moth known is the nepticulid moth, which is about the size of a pinhead. Many insects are so small we can't even see them with the naked eye. Dust mites invade almost every inch of our world, and we can't even see them. But if you have allergies, they sure can make you sneeze!

easily. When a victim approaches, the spider pounces upon it, shooting it with poison. Then, the spider drags the victim down into its burrow and eats it. The trapdoor spider isn't the only sneaky designer of homes. Tiger beetle larvae will also dig a nice trap in the dirt, where it lies waiting for the next passerby. Similarly, the larvae of the ant lion does the same, but it prefers sand to soil. And if it seems like the wait is taking too long, the impatient ant lion will spit sand at a passing ant and knock it down into the pit.

## Spitting Ladybugs

How can it be that those cute little ladybugs like to misbehave and spit? Well, maybe they don't really spit—they ooze! And it's very un-ladybug-like, if you think about it. But it's true. Ladybugs (also known as *ladybird bugs*) are one of the friendliest bugs around. So what makes them spit or ooze? Fear. They are afraid of being eaten or harmed and rely on ooze for self-defense. If a bird catches a ladybug for lunch, it just might take a rain check on its meal if the ladybug releases its smelly, bad tasting ooze from its legs. If you don't mind being oozed on and want to see how this works, you can do it without harming the ladybug. Just lay it on its back and very gently press on it, as if you were going to squeeze it. Once the ladybug realizes that it's in danger, it will ooze right onto your hand. (After you finish this experiment, be sure you wash your hands to get rid of that stinky stuff!)

## Dangerous Bugs

Bugging a bug can be downright bogus—and dangerous! Messing with some insects can be deadly. What will an insect do to win a battle with a predator? A dragonfly nymph juts out its jaw of hooks, piercing its opponent, while a puss moth

# Terribly Tiny

A mite is a teensy, tiny creature related to a spider. Even though you have never seen them, there are bunches of mites living very close to you. Up to 25 mites at a time can cram themselves head-first into this very small space. They eat during the day, and at night wiggle out to mate and lay their eggs. Use the decoder to learn where these common mites like to hide. Be careful—do you really want to know?

Where are they?!

| B | | G | | N | | T | |
|---|---|---|---|---|---|---|---|
| A ◣◢ D | | F ◣◢ H | | M ╳ O | | S ╳ U | |
| E | | L | | R | | Y | |

caterpillar whips its tail and spits acid at its attackers. The black bulldog ant can get really mean. It not only bites, but it also stings its attacker at the same time. And the yellowtail moth can give you a rash if you touch its hairs. The darkling beetle has this trick up its sleeve: It will stand on its head and spray a fluid all over its would-be predator. The sawfly gums its attacker or prey to death. The scorpion strikes those who threaten it with the telson, a spike at the end of its tail.

Earwigs use their horned feelers (antennae at the end of their tails) to protect their eggs and young. Some caterpillars simply poison anyone who touches them with their venom-filled hairs. Aphids kick small wasps that try to bother them. Crickets wrestle and bite their opponents to death. Horsefly larvae drag the tiny toads that come too close down into the mud and suck all of the juices out of their bodies. The bombardier beetle bombs or sprays its attackers with a gas. This gas removes all the oxygen they need from the air, so that they are unable to breath. Then they stop dead in their tracks. (And guess what? This is how fire extinguishers work too: they provide a rush of gas to get rid of any oxygen, so the fire can't keep going.)

Bugs that prey on animals for blood have a special mouth shaped like a straw, which they use to puncture the skin and slurp up the blood. These straw mouths are very handy. Have you ever tried to drink a milkshake without a straw? You wouldn't get very far, would you? Of course, you can always just skip the milkshake and eat a burger and French fries! But most of these bugs survive on liquid meals. Here's what a fly does, for instance: It spits on food first and then waits for it to dissolve so that it can slurp it up with its straw mouth.

# Water Slide

**Follow this bug called a "pond skater" across the water from START to END.
Remember—don't cross the lily pads!**

START

END

# APPENDIX
# Puzzle Answers

### page 3 • Picture in the Sky

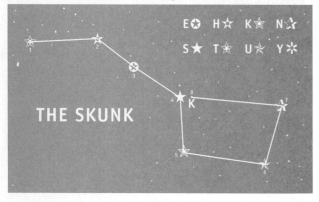

E✪  H☆  K☆  N☆
S★  T☆  U☆  Y❊

THE SKUNK

### page 5 • The Big Bucket

*The bucket would have to be more than this many miles wide!*

### page 8 • Crazy Moon

L U N A T I C

### page 11 • Go to Jail

*He proved that the earth was not the center of the solar system.*

## page 18 • Many Meerkats

The total of all the numbers in the picture is 108. Since there are 12 meerkats (including the babies), each meerkat gets 9.

## page 27 • Pony Express

## page 25 • Gentle Giants

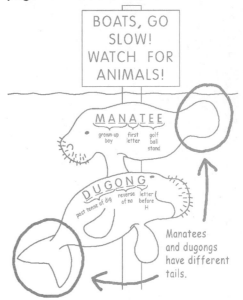

BOATS, GO SLOW! WATCH FOR ANIMALS!

MANATEE
grown-up boy / first letter / golf ball stand

DUGONG
past tense of dig / reverse of no / letter before H

Manatees and dugongs have different tails.

## page 43 • Game Pieces

fly ball

southpaw

home run

bullpen

page 45 • Where's the Player?

What is the difference between a football player and a duck?

You'll find one in a huddle, and the other in a puddle!

page 51 • Find the Football

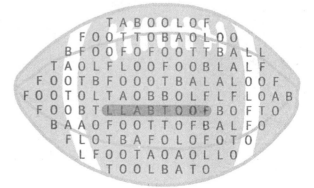

page 53 • Keep Your Eye on the Ball

page 57 • Ptiny Pterosaurs

## page 59 • Full Plates

STEGOSNORUS

What do you call a dinosaur who makes noise as he sleeps?

ZZZZ

## page 61 • Keep Looking

## page 62 • Why Did the Dinosaur Cross the Road?

Because chickens had not evolved yet!

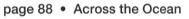

## page 88 • Across the Ocean

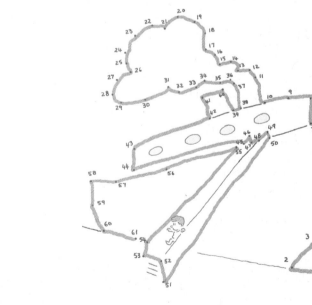

### page 91 • Living Dangerously

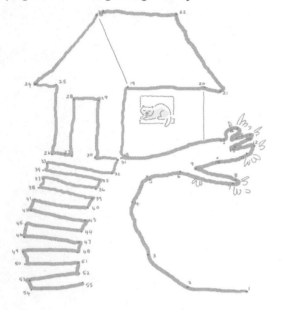

### page 95 • Mini Mountain

### page 97 • Longest Largest

Yangtze (China): 3,917 miles
Yellow (China): 3,398 miles
Lena (Russia): 2,736 miles
Volga (Russia): 2,266 miles
Indus (Pakistan and India): 1,976 miles

The Yangtze is often called the
dirtiest river in Asia.

### page 101 • Maple Magic

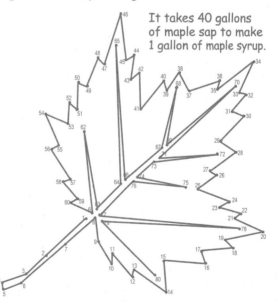

It takes 40 gallons
of maple sap to make
1 gallon of maple syrup.

## page 105 • You Live Where?

Bacon 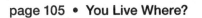, TX

Wink 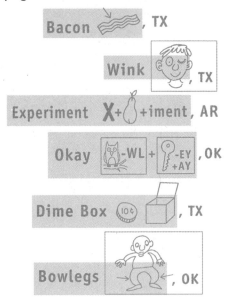, TX

Experiment X+🍐+iment, AR

Okay 🦉-WL + 🔑-EY +AY, OK

Dime Box 10¢ 📦, TX

Bowlegs 🧍, OK

## page 108 • Pickles?

| POMEGRANATES | ~~PEAS~~ | PAPAYAS |
| PARSNIPS | (PEANUTS) | ~~PEARS~~ |
| (PECANS) | PENCILS | PEPPERS |
| PALMETTOS | PIMENTOS | PUMPKINS |
| ~~PASTA~~ | ~~PICKLES~~ | PRETZELS |
| POPCORN | ~~PORK~~ | ~~PORCUPINES~~ |
| PAPRIKA | PENNIES | ~~PLOWS~~ |
| ~~PATIOS~~ | ~~POTATOES~~ | (PEACHES) |
| PICKLES | ~~ROSES~~ | ~~PANTHERS~~ |
| ~~PLUMS~~ | PETUNIAS | ~~PANCAKES~~ |

## page 106 • One to Grow On

## page 116 • Hiding in a Honeycomb

ant, bee, beetle, fly, flea, ladybug

## page 119 • What's the Difference?

What's the difference between a coyote and a flea?

| | T | E | | | | Y | | | | | O | |
| T | N | E | | R | A | P | R | | | | | O | |
| O | R | | I | H | I | E | R | A | W | O | S | | T | E |
| P | H | H | E | H | O | | L | S | N | L | N | T | H | N | E |
| O | N | E | | H | O | W | L | S | | O | N | | T | H | E |
| P | R | A | I | R | I | E | | A | N | D | | T | H | E |
| O | T | H | E | R | | P | R | O | W | L | S | | O | N |
| T | H | E | | H | A | I | R | Y |

**page 121 • Feed Me**

**page 124 • Got Maggots?**

JUGGLER
FOGGY
DRAGGED
EGGROLL
HUGGED
BIGGER
GIGGLE
BAGGAGE
WIGGLE
SUGGEST
NUGGET

**page 127 • Arachnophobia**

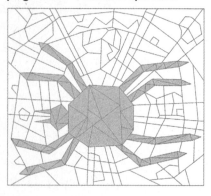

**page 131 • Water Slide**

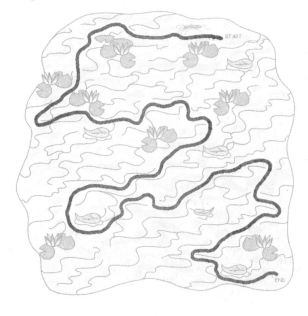

**page 129 • Terribly Tiny**

AROUND THE
ROOTS OF YOUR
EYELASHES.
YES, YOURS!

# We Have
# EVERYTHING®
## on Anything!

**With more than 19 million** copies sold, the Everything® series has become one of America's favorite resources for solving problems, learning new skills, and organizing lives. Our brand is not only recognizable—it's also welcomed.

The series is a hand-in-hand partner for people who are ready to tackle new subjects—like you!

For more information on the Everything® series, please visit *www.adamsmedia.com*

The Everything® list spans a wide range of subjects, with more than 500 titles covering 25 different categories:

| | | |
|---|---|---|
| Business | History | Reference |
| Careers | Home Improvement | Religion |
| Children's Storybooks | Everything Kids | Self-Help |
| Computers | Languages | Sports & Fitness |
| Cooking | Music | Travel |
| Crafts and Hobbies | New Age | Wedding |
| Education/Schools | Parenting | Writing |
| Games and Puzzles | Personal Finance | |
| Health | Pets | |